M000281195

ILLEGITIMATE
SUN

HOW A NAVAL CRYPTOLOGIST CRACKED THE CODE OF LIFE LESSONS

Copyright © 2021 KennethEarl26 Publishing and Consulting Services

All rights reserved. No part of this publication may be reproduced, distributed, or transmitted in any form or by any means, including photocopying, recording, or other electronic or mechanical methods, without the prior written permission of the publisher, except in the case of brief quotations embodied in critical reviews and certain other noncommercial uses permitted by copyright law. For permission requests, write to the publisher, addressed "Attention: Permissions Coordinator," at the address below.

KennethEarl26 Publishing and Consulting Services
10325 Kensington Pkwy
Kensington, MD 20891-2094

http://www.illegitimate-sun.com
KennethEarlt26@gmail.com

ISBN: 978-1-7375650-2-4 (hardcover)
ISBN: 978-1-7375650-0-0 (paperback)
ISBN: 978-1-7375650-1-7 (ebook)

Ordering Information:
Special discounts are available on quantity purchases by corporations, associations, and others. For details, contact PO Box 2370 10325 Kensington Pkwy Kensington, MD 20891-2370 or email KennethEarlt26@gmail.com.

ILLEGITIMATE SUN

HOW A NAVAL CRYPTOLOGIST CRACKED THE CODE OF LIFE LESSONS

A SPY MEMOIR

KENNETH EARL

DEDICATION

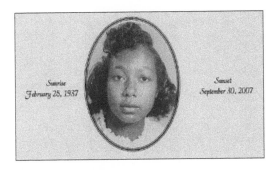

Sunrise
February 28, 1937

Sunset
September 30, 2007

To honor my mother, I wrote this book to give back what was given to me, the legacy of her character.

THE JOURNEY

Disclaimer: The views expressed in this book are the author's own and do not imply endorsement by the Office of the Director of National Intelligence (ODNI) or any other U.S. Government agency. This book does not contain any classified, codeword, or other sensitive information. All referenced source materials were derived from unclassified information available to the general public.

CHAPTER 1

WELCOME TO THE SPY WORLD

Drug Enforcement Administration (DEA)
Headquarters, Arlington, Virginia

"The purpose of life, as far as I can tell…is to find a mode of being that is so meaningful that the fact that life is suffering is no longer relevant."
—Jordan B. Peterson

On a Wednesday afternoon in the summer of 2010, I was standing near a river birch tree at the front entrance of the U.S. Drug Enforcement Administration (DEA) headquarters in Arlington, Virginia, near the Pentagon. I was awaiting the other members of our counterintelligence and cybersecurity risk assessment team having been the first to exit the building following our classified meeting.

This was at the height of the global war on terrorism following the September 11 attacks, where 19 terrorists hijacked four airplanes and killed nearly 3,000 people in New York, Washington, D.C., and Pennsylvania. Our country, and our world, were still experi-

Drug Enforcement Administration (DEA) Headquarters Building,
Army-Navy Drive, Arlington, Virginia.

encing the anguish and pain of those horrible events. At the same time, there were U.S. and foreign espionage and spy operations lurking in the shadows.

On this particular afternoon, my team and I, along with our director and principal deputy, had just conducted an official classified debriefing with the drug enforcement administrator and her most senior DEA officials. The debrief examined counterintelligence, cybersecurity threats, and risks to the DEA special agents serving in two countries on two separate continents. Due to the extremely sensitive nature of the mission, the locations and the details of our work remain classified to this day to protect the sources, methods, and operations that DEA special agents conduct globally. However, a 2010 National Drug Threat Assessment Report from the U.S. Department of Justice[1] does outline the general impact of drug trafficking organizations and the threat they pose to the United States.

At the time, we were government officials for the Office of the National Counterintelligence Executive, now named the National Counterintelligence and Security Center, which falls under the Office of the Director of National Intelligence. A post created in the wake of the September 11 attacks, the Director of National Intelligence (DNI) is the top intelligence official in the United States government. The DNI oversees the U.S. intelligence community, which consists of 16 civilian and military agencies including the Central Intelligence Agency (CIA), the Defense Intelligence Agency (DIA), the Federal Bureau of Investigation (FBI), the National Security Agency (NSA), the Drug Enforcement Administration (DEA), each of the U.S. military services, and other agencies.

Office of Director National Intelligence (ODNI) Seal.

The team I led was largely made up of retired high-level Senior Executive Service and Senior Executive Intelligence Service officials

---

1   U.S. Department of Justice, National Drug Intelligence Center, National Drug Threat Assessment (2010) https://www.justice.gov/archive/ndic/pubs38/38661/38661p.pdf.

with more than 25 years of counterespionage and special agent experience gained from working in the CIA, FBI, Naval Criminal Investigative Service, Army Military Intelligence, and Air Force Office of Special Investigations. All of whom were now government contractors and consultants for the intelligence community. Basically, they were experienced spycatchers. Each member of the team was older than me and very accomplished. I referred to them as the *greybeards* because of their extensive wisdom, knowledge, and experience of U.S. intelligence, counterintelligence, and law enforcement.

The intelligence community as a whole was remarkably busy that summer of 2010 with the aforementioned global war on terrorism and with the investigation of the Illegals Program,[2] a network of Russian sleeper agents. This investigation, called Operation Ghost Stories, culminated with the arrest of 10 people in the U.S. and an eleventh in Cyprus, at the end of June 2010. The arrested spies were Russian nationals, most of whom were using false identities, who had been planted in the U.S. by the Russian Foreign Intelligence Service. Posing as ordinary American citizens, they tried to build contacts with academics, industrialists, and policymakers to gain access to intelligence. They were the target of a multi-year investigation by the FBI. The sleeper agents were charged with carrying out long-term, 'deep cover' assignments in the United States on behalf of the Russian Federation.

Some of these sleeper agents went so far as to get married and have children together to cultivate and maintain their covert identities. Federal district courts alleged the agents passed secret messages to the Russian Foreign Intelligence Service using methods such

2 Illegals Program. Operation Ghost Stories: Inside the Russian Spy Case — FBI (2011)

as disappearing ink, shortwave radio transmissions, digital photographs and more. Some agents even traded messages by swapping identical bags while passing each other in train stations.

So, what was their purpose? At the time, the Russian Federation was interested in learning more about U.S. policy in Central America. They were also interested in learning more about U.S. interpretation of Russian foreign policy, and U.S. strategy on the use of the internet by terrorist groups.

Several members of our team of greybeards had conducted similar espionage investigations to Operation Ghost Stories, that also impacted national security. These cases sometimes involved U.S. spies—for example, Aldrich Ames, Robert Hanssen, and John Walker Jr., among others that are not so well known.

Ames was a former CIA officer turned KGB double agent. For years, Ames used his position as a CIA officer to spy on the U.S. for the Soviet Union and Russia. Ames started off passing along what he thought was harmless information for a fee. But once he rang that bell, he could not un-ring it. Before long, he began betraying intelligence assets—real people—for cash. Agents started to disappear. CIA officials eventually realized there was a mole in the agency. In March 1993, the CIA and FBI began an intensive investigation of Ames. From November 1993 until his arrest, Ames was kept under virtually constant physical surveillance. He was convicted of espionage in 1994.[3]

Robert Hanssen, a veteran FBI counterintelligence agent, was arrested in 2001 and charged with espionage on the behalf of the

---

3   "Aldrich Ames." FBI, May 18, 2016. https://www.fbi.gov/history/famous-cases/
     aldrich-ames.

intelligence services of the former Soviet Union. According to the FBI, Hanssen provided extensive highly classified national security information to the Russians. The arrest affidavit alleged that Hanssen had, on at least 20 separate occasions, left packages at dead drop sites in the Washington D.C. area for the KGB and its successor, the SVR. In total, Hanssen gave the Russians more than 6,000 pages of valuable material. That material comprised dozens of classified documents, including "top secret" and "codeword" details, as well as critical information on technical operations. Ultimately, it compromised numerous human sources in the U.S. intelligence community. Hanssen also revealed FBI counterintelligence investigation techniques, sources, methods, and operations. According to the affidavit, Hanssen provided the intel in exchange for diamonds and cash worth more than $600,000.[4]

John Walker Jr., like me, served and retired from the U.S. Navy. He was a chief warrant officer and radioman (communications specialist) during his time in the Navy. But from 1968 to 1985, he was also spying for the Soviet Union.

Walker helped the Soviets decipher more than one million encrypted naval messages. He put together a spy ring, which included a close friend of his, a brother, and even his own son, that he maintained after his retirement from the Navy. In 1987, The *New York Times* dubbed it "the most damaging Soviet spy ring in history."[5] The greybeards involved in these cases were experienced spy catchers. Although I was extremely confident about the briefing and

---

4   "Robert Hanssen." FBI, May 18, 2016. https://www.fbi.gov/history/famous-cases/robert-hanssen.

5   "August 2019: John Anthony Walker, Jr.. Spy Case." FBI, January 25, 2021. https://www.fbi.gov/history/artifact-of-the-month/august-2019-john-anthony-walker-jr-spy-case.

work we had just completed, this had been my first opportunity to lead an assessment of this level of magnitude that literally impacted global operations and our national security. So, I was anxious to learn what the greybeards thought of the debriefing. This was an important meeting with DEA officials where we were to discuss imminent and ongoing threats to the DEA special agents operating in these two extremely dangerous regions of the world. Think of the transnational criminal organizations and drug gangs who perpetrate violence globally and, in our country, those who terrorize citizens through death, fear, and intimidation. We were there to discuss the impact of these activities on our U.S. national security and safety—to assess the situation and advise the DEA officials on our findings to better support and protect our operations.

The DEA is responsible for taking on drug trafficking and distribution within the U.S. It shares jurisdiction with the FBI, U.S. Immigration and Customs Enforcement, the Department of Homeland Security, and more. It coordinates and pursues drug investigations both domestically and abroad. That often means that DEA agents are in close contact with powerful and dangerous people.

In 2010, the DEA had 83 offices in 62 countries, with personnel working to assess drug threats, gather intelligence, and target major drug trafficking organizations. Heroin, marijuana, methamphetamine, and cocaine dominated the market.

At the time, violence in Mexico was a major concern. Gun battles between law enforcement, criminals, and rival traffickers were commonplace. During those times, traffickers employed methods intended to intimidate police and undermine the public's trust in law enforcement through corruption. It was not unusual to see stories on the news covering the discovery of mass graves, executions, and decapitations of rivals, all for the public to see.[6]

Before long, the team emerged from the building. I stayed rooted to my spot near the river birch tree, scanning their faces for any hints they might reveal, and I was nervously optimistic. I was recalling how the DEA administrator, in the middle of the debriefing, had summoned several DEA officials to the conference room to hear the recommendations we were outlining on the spot. Her reaction had been a powerful display of leadership, and showed her concern that her senior leadership team should be made aware, as a matter of urgency, of the important information we were providing about current operations, cybersecurity threats, and counterintelligence risks in the locations we were debriefing. I felt fairly confident as I stood there with these thoughts racing through my mind, but I was still uncertain because these greybeards were always tough, very thorough, extraordinarily unapologetic, and stoic. Not necessarily a very *fun* group of men.

Suddenly, one of the greybeards, a former FBI executive and a Washington D.C. homicide commander, rushed towards me. He gave me a long embrace, stepped back, and shook my hand. I was stunned.

"That was totally outstanding," he said. "You did a great job. What an impactful briefing."

Though his words were as plain and simple, trust me, they were unprecedented. This greybeard had *never* recognized or acknowledged my efforts before, let alone praised my work, ever!

---

6   https://www.dea.gov/sites/default/files/pr/speeches-testimony/2012-2009/100505_
     inc.pdf

Now, that was not because my work up until that point had been anything other than exceptional. By all accounts, it was. But this greybeard had seen a lot in his many years as a special agent for the FBI and as the head of D.C. Homicide. To him, I was still inexperienced in this area of spy catching, espionage, and investigations, a viewpoint which was valid because I was a naval cryptologist by trade—the cyber guy leading the assessment. He thought I was still wet behind the ears and needed to earn my stripes before I gained his respect.

He was a close friend and confidant of our director of the Office of the National Counterintelligence Executive who was himself a previous deputy director of the FBI, the number two guy at the Bureau. So, his acknowledgement and reaction felt like a full endorsement and recognition by all. But this greybeard had no trouble repeatedly saying to me, "Stop self-congratulating, you haven't done anything yet!"

As someone who had started as a cryptologist in the U.S. Navy, I had found success along the way and took opportunities and moments to celebrate on occasion. But this work and environment was different. I was not protecting secured classified communications systems or working with foreign language interpreters or signal intelligence analysts. I was working with human intelligence assets, freaking *spies*, some of whom were once undercover double agents. That meant we did not celebrate because the mission is never over when human intelligence spies are involved, and where operations could still go terribly wrong in the counterintelligence and espionage environments.

But in this case, and on this occasion, he actually hugged me, and I *knew* he was proud of my efforts and our accomplishments together. The job was done. But even more than that, his embrace signaled, "Welcome to the spy world, Mr. Earl, we accept you."

This was a gratifying moment for me. It was difficult to earn the praise and respect of these spy-world greybeards and cold war warriors—it felt like hell sometimes.

So, where did this all start? How did I get to this point to working with the greybeards, top espionage and law enforcement officials? Well, this is the story of the Illegitimate Sun.

CHAPTER 2

WISDOM AND INTEGRITY

Cherry Street, Columbia, South Carolina

"Wisdom is knowing the right path to take. Integrity is taking it."
—M.H. McKee

I was the fourth of four children, born to an unwed mother who was living in a small, two-bedroom wooden house on Cherry Street in the early 1960s. The street lay in an underprivileged neighborhood in the state capital of Columbia, South Carolina, where many African Americans were the working poor, and often lived below the poverty line.

We lived next door to my grandparents, Pappy and Sugg. My grandfather did under-the-table construction work while my grandmother was a housemaid and cook for a wealthy, white southern family. Neither of my grandparents had a formal education.

My sister and I on Cherry Street, Columbia, South Carolina—1968.

My mother, Florence Marie, had to drop out of high school when she became pregnant with my oldest brother, but she did eventually earn her general education diploma. My mom was proud, wise, perceptive, and determined, but like many poor, disadvantaged African-American families in the South, she encountered social, economic, educational, and racial barriers; it was hard living in those times. This was doubly true for an unwed mother with four children.

Born In 1937, following the Great Depression and during the Jim Crow era, my mother demonstrated personal fortitude, self-reliance, determination, character, and integrity. Jim Crow laws were a collection of state and local statutes that legalized racial segregation. Named after an African-American minstrel show character, Jim Crow laws were in place from just after the Civil War and were meant to marginalize African Americans by denying them the right to vote, hold jobs, get an education, and have access to other opportunities.

The roots of Jim Crow laws can be seen as early as 1865, immediately following the ratification of the 13th Amendment of the Constitution, which abolished slavery in the United States. During those times, as you can imagine, my grandparents raised my mother and her two older siblings through extraordinary difficulty. You see, my mother's parents were both children of sharecroppers[7] and their parents were only one generation removed from slavery itself. African-American codes existed during their youth and life as parents. These were strict local and state laws that detailed when, where and how formerly enslaved people could work, and for how much compensation. The codes were a legal way of putting African-American citizens into indentured servitude, to deny them voting rights, to control where they lived and how they traveled, and to seize children for labor purposes. This meant that segregated waiting rooms in bus and train stations were required, as were segregated spaces at water fountains, restrooms, building entrances, elevators, cemeteries, and even amusement-park cashier windows.

School Days
1944-45

My mother, Florence Marie, during her school days in the Jim Crow era—1945.

7   Sharecropper/Sharecropping is a type of farming in which families rent small plots of land from a landowner in return for a portion of their crop, to be given to the landowner at the end of each year. In the rural south, it was typically practiced by former slaves. In the early years most African Americans in rural areas of the South were left without land and forced to work as laborers on large white-owned farms and plantations to earn a living.
Sources: The Rise and Fall of Jim Crow. Richard Wormser; Segregated America. Smithsonian Institute. https://www.history.com/topics/early-20th-century-us/jim-crow-laws Access Date March 1, 2020 Publisher A&E Television Networks. Last Updated February 21, 2020. Original Published Date February 28, 2018

It was not until 1948 that President Harry Truman ordered the desegregation of the military, and only in 1954 did the Supreme Court rule in *Brown v. Board of Education* that educational segregation was unconstitutional, ending the era of separate-but-equal education. In 1964, President Lyndon B. Johnson signed the Civil Rights Act, which legally ended the segregation that had been institutionalized by the Jim Crow laws. And in 1965, the Voting Rights Act halted efforts to keep minorities from voting. The Fair Housing Act of 1968, which ended discrimination in renting and selling homes, followed.

These were richly complicated and tough times for African Americans, but my grandparents and mother all were determined to create a better life for themselves and their children.

African-American school children posing with their teacher outside a segregated one-room school, in South Carolina—1905.

My mother started work as a cook in the kitchen of Dorn Veterans Affairs Medical Center Hospital in Columbia, which was about a four-mile walk from Cherry Street. She worked her way up over the years, eventually becoming a well-respected nursing assistant. She earned the esteem and admiration of all the nurses, doctors, and veterans at the Center, and she had many friends who genuinely loved and cared deeply about her. Despite her circumstances, challenges, and barriers in life, my mother was a believer in God, self-reliance, character, and integrity.

In the early days, we attended First Nazareth Baptist Church on the corner of Gervais Street and Millwood Avenue, mere walking distance from our house on Cherry Street. I recall the day, when I was five years old, that my mother took us all to the altar to join the church. I remember kicking and screaming as we walked down the church aisle, I was so afraid of all the people staring at me. I am not sure if I was embarrassed or afraid. Despite my antics, we joined the church that day. A few Sundays later, my siblings and I were baptized in the icy-cold water.

My mother was an avid Bible reader, particularly the Psalms and Proverbs. She often wrote verses down on notepaper and I would find them in various places in her bedroom, on mirrors, in books, and she quoted them regularly, many of her favorites focused on faith and strength.

Though money was tight, and we fell well below the poverty line, I did not really know or understand at that time that we were poor because every Christmas or Thanksgiving, my mother would fill the house full of relatives to enjoy gifts, good food and good company. People were full of excitement then, even though there was not much room to move around. We would find ourselves stepping over each other and fighting for space on the couch, but we did not mind. I especially loved when my aunts, uncles, and cousins would visit from New Jersey, New York, and Maryland.

We were full and happy. My mother made these mustard greens I just loved. She also made peach pies, baked ham, cornbread, and candied yams. She was a great cook, and the food was always delicious. I cannot even imagine packing that many people into that house now, but I remember feeling grateful and genuinely cared for.

By the time I had turned five years old, in 1968, my mom had worked hard and was able to buy a recently built gray stone house in a much nicer neighborhood in the Farrow Hills community of Columbia. Yes, times were still hard, but she was determined to provide my siblings and me with a better home and opportunities through the example she was setting of hard work and taking accountability. Increasingly, I discovered my mother was fearless. She had many friends, and I have come to learn that her strength and courage were a big part of the reason why. Her raw and unapologetic words and thoughts—and very colorful language— drew people in.

During my youth, many of my friends thought my mother was strict and harsh, which was true, but there was much more underneath the surface of her brashness. She was real, compassionate, astute, and empathetic.

Moving to a new neighborhood was quite the adjustment for me. Many of the families living there were what I would consider lower- to middle-class African Americans, in mostly two-parent households. The neighborhood on Cherry Street had been quite different, where many were considered the working poor and were less educated, relatively speaking. This perceived difference became apparent soon enough. The school I attended in the new neighborhood had partnered with the county and the City of Columbia's Scared Straight program for so-called at-risk youth. Though, generally, I was a good kid (or so I thought), the school singled me out, along with some other kids, and volunteered my participation into the program.   Of course, my mother had to agree to allow me to attend this all-day program of instruction at the city jail. The program was designed to scare youth into making better decisions and to avoid going to jail. They used correction officials and real prisoners to provide instruction, stories, and testimonies of experiences and their criminal behavior. There was a tour of the jail facility which was *really scary* to experience for a sixth grader. Some of it was an act, but when you are a kid, you do not know that. It terrified me enough that I resolved right then and there never to get into trouble or go to jail.

I was not a bad kid. I was even in the Boy Scouts for a while. However, although not as tough as Cherry Street, the Farrow Hills neighborhood presented different challenges and I had to learn how to defend myself early on. I recall this bully, let us call him B.J. This B.J. used to take my lunch money all the time and bully other kids. I was afraid to tell my mother and older brothers, but I would be hungry at school because B.J. had taken my means to buy lunch. I accepted the situation as a fact of life. But one day, I decided I was tired of being bullied. As I walked to school and passed B.J. at the top of the hill, he said, as he always did, "Give it up."

I said, "No, not today."

As he reached for my pockets, I punched him in the face, knocking him to the ground. That was the last time he ever tried to bully me or take my lunch money. Of course, as an adult, I do not condone violence of any kind, but in the moment and as a 10-year-old, I believed I had to stand up for myself.

Though my mother and brothers were unaware of my trials in the new neighborhood, I am certain they would have approved of me standing up for myself. My mother was strong, and her opinion meant everything to me both as a child and as a young man. Even now, I am driven to honor her legacy and do the right things in her memory.

So, it was doubly hard when I *did* disappoint her. Other than being mischievous, the worst thing I ever did as a kid was wreck my mom's new car. One day, as I waited for her to finish getting dressed so she could drop me off at school and head to work, I jumped behind the steering wheel as if I were driving. At the time, I was 11 years old. I accidently put the gear shift in neutral and the car rolled off the carport, knocked down the neighbor's mailbox and crashed into a large tree.

My mother heard the loud noise, came to the front door, and saw the car. Not yet fully dressed, she ran across the street to survey the damage. There was a big dent in the back of the trunk. She picked up a branch that had fallen from the tree and instantly began to discipline me, I mean, it was a beat-down in front of the neighbors, and she then made me walk to school. She drove around with that big dent in the car for a long time, and it was only later that I realized it was because she did not have auto insurance or out-of-pocket cash to repair the damage to the trunk. Two or so years later, she had saved enough to purchase a new car.

My mother always did the best she could to take care of us four kids on her own. Even today, at this point in my life, I would not look back and change a thing about how we grew up.

I never had any substantive discussions with my mother about my father. I do recall asking her about him once when she was helping me finish some application paperwork for either school or the Navy. I asked her why she had left the space for her maiden name blank. "I don't want to talk about that," she said. Though my mother was strong and transparent, I saw an expression on her face that surprised me. I could see the hurt, or maybe shame, in her eyes. It was clear to me that she did not want to discuss why she never married and was unwedded with four children.

"It's okay, Mom, I understand," I said.

And because I never, ever wanted to cause her hurt, pain, or shame, the conversation ended there, and I never brought it up again. My mother is the best example of courage and resilience I have observed over my lifetime. Even in death, she remains my true hero. It was because of her that I developed the character and temperament I have today.

She is my guiding light and strength. To have seen how she accomplished the nearly impossible in her life and at the same time gain the respect and admiration of others has been inspiring and I credit her for how I am able to make effective life choices and professional career decisions based on my own natural instincts, character, honesty, and integrity.

As I reflect on the many conversations my mother and I had, I recall the first time she explained the Golden Rule. I was about seven or eight years old, and I had mentioned to my mom that I really did not like this kid at my school in our new neighborhood.

Showing no empathy for me, she said, "Kenneth, do unto others as you would have them do unto you."

Confused and unclear on what she meant, I said, "Mom, I do not understand."

She responded with, "In other words, son, treat people like you would want to be treated, that is the Golden Rule." This was the first life lesson she taught me and has remained a constant in my life ever since.

By 1978, my two older brothers had graduated from high school and joined the military. My oldest brother had joined the U.S. Air Force and my second brother had joined the U.S. Army. My sister went off to college. So, during my final three years of high school, it was just my mother and I still at home. My sister was set to be the first to graduate college in my immediate family, however, I saw firsthand the financial strain that a college education had put on her and my mother. Ronald Reagan was president, and the U.S. economy was entering a recession with a growing unemployment rate. I knew if I did not obtain an athletic scholarship to pay for college, the military would be my only alternative.

I thought for sure I would receive a few college offers given I was a varsity basketball star and a leading scorer at W.J. Keenan High School. Both my brothers were good at football too, and my middle brother even lettered in four sports in one year; he was quite the athlete. But for me, the athletic scholarships never came, and I was initially a bit a dejected. But later, my basketball coach, Dr. Carlos Smith, a military veteran, told me that he had played basketball at a high level while serving in the U.S. Army. He suggested that I think about joining the military where I could have a career, obtain an education, play basketball, travel the world, and serve my country. He sold it as an all-in-one package, and I was convinced.

But what really sealed the deal was my best friend, Wayne Sinkler. Following my meeting with Coach Smith, Wayne came up to me in the hallway at school all excited, and he informed me that he and our mutual friend and classmate, Myron Jones, had signed up to join the Navy.

"Do you want to join?" he asked.

"Do I have to know how to swim?"

"I don't know, but I can't swim either," he said.

Days later, I officially entered the Navy's Delayed Entry Program, and because I was under the age of 18, my mother signed the application paperwork. In addition to my military aptitude test, the Navy recruiter requested that I take a Defense Language Aptitude Battery (DLAB) test; I scored high and was officially placed on a contract to become a naval cryptologist as a Russian linguist.

CHAPTER 3

SELF-DISCOVERY

Defense Language Institute (DLI),
Monterey, California

"Life is an endless process of self-discovery."
—John W. Gardner

It was November 1981 when I arrived at the San Francisco International Airport, following a summer of fun with my friends and family after my high school graduation, and then eight weeks of basic Navy recruit training in Orlando, Florida.

In California, being out west, something just felt different, since I had never before left the East Coast. I remember feeling a sense of wonder as I walked through the airport, seeing an array of nationalities, professionals, hair colors, and the like. I saw many men and women dressed in business suits, and several like punk rockers with rainbow mohawk haircuts.

It was a vastly different experience and feeling from the much smaller Columbia Metropolitan Airport in South Carolina. Strolling through the busy terminal, I could smell freshly baked bread as I people watched and listened to the flight announcements. I then retrieved my Navy sea bag from the baggage claim and headed towards the ground transportation area to the bus terminal to take the 110-mile, three-and-a-half-hour bus ride, with multiple stops along the way, to my destination of Monterey, California. Given the time difference of three hours from the East Coast, I was excited to know that I would have a full day of sunlight to enjoy the trip and the extraordinarily scenic views, and I found myself transfixed by what I saw outside the bus window.

San Francisco International Airport terminal.

Headed south, I caught glimpses of the San Francisco Bay, and the cities of Palo Alto, San Jose, and Santa Cruz. Soon, the highway gave way to mountains and landscape like I had never seen in South Carolina, or any place on the East Coast. I was already in awe of the place when we broke through the mountains and followed the coast of Monterey Bay to the Presidio—the military base where I would spend the next eight months of my life.

The Presidio of Monterey is an active U.S. Army installation with historic ties to the Spanish colonial era and it is the home of the Defense Language Institute Foreign Language Center. There was certainly nothing like this in the neighborhood where I grew up. The name alone was enough to make an impression on me but actually seeing and being on the installation was awe-inspiring.

The installation overlooked magnificent cliffs and had a view of the Monterey Bay. The bright blue water lapped relentlessly at the rocks and churned out sea foam. Because of its high altitude, a thick fog always seemed to hang in the air, like we were touching the clouds. It was beautiful. It felt almost magical.

This small base was teeming with civilian students and personnel of all branches of the military, including the Army, Navy, Air Force, Marines, and even the CIA, FBI, and State Department, all there to learn foreign languages and culture. Native speakers taught Russian, Chinese/Mandarin, French, Korean, and Arabic, among other languages and dialects.

I came to Monterey with the expectation that I would learn Russian. That was, after all, in the terms of my original contract which had been based on the scores from my language aptitude test. But there was a change of plans. I was placed on the Korean language course instead. The Navy course manager explained to me that the Cold War with Russia was ending, and that the Navy needed more Korean linguists to support U.S. national interests. He shared the story of the USS Pueblo (AGER-2) incident.[8] The Pueblo was an environmental research ship, attached to naval intelligence as a spy ship, that was captured by North Korean forces. The North Kore-

8   USS Pueblo (AGER-2) Incident. http://www.usspueblo.org/

ans had then reverse-engineered the communications devices and had therefore gained access to the cryptographic encryption keys used on the Pueblo, which allowed the North Koreans to potentially decrypt and read classified transmissions. I was captivated by the story and would soon learn more about North Korean history.

USS Pueblo (AGER-2) shown here underway at sea was captured by North Korean patrol boats and taken to Wonson. There were 83 men reported aboard. January 23, 1968.

Though I was excited to get started, I recall being nervous because I was told that Korean was among the more difficult languages to grasp, and the attrition rate was relatively high. In the early days, my initial impression of the native Korean instructors was that they were assertive, and the language tone and mannerisms seemed abrupt, at least to me. English was rarely, if ever, spoken in the classroom setting. A typical morning greeting between my Korean instructor and I would be as follows:

안녕하세요 Mr. Earl. 오늘 어떠세요?

저는 훌륭한 성 교사입니다. 아침은 어때?

훌륭 해요, 고맙습니다. 시작하자.

Translation:

"Good Morning Mr. Earl. How are you today?"

"I am fine, Instructor Seong. How is your morning?"

"Excellent, thank you. Let's get started."

Each class had a military and/or civilian advisor to assist and support its students before and after classroom sessions.

We had to learn at least 100 new words per week. We were issued cassette players, tape recordings of Korean language speakers, and headphones so we could listen to the language and therefore practice our speaking, reading, and writing skills. But the training went deeper than speaking, reading, and writing. We had to learn the context of the language, cultural information, and some North Korean history, which included the war between North and South Korea, and the Pueblo incident. Coincidentally, I later served on the USS Chosin (CG-65), which was named after the *Battle of Chosin Reservoir*, an important battle in the Korean War.

I attended class for six hours a day and had to study for two to three hours during the evening. It was not something I was accustomed to. It would have been rigorous for anyone, but I had to study overtime to compensate because I had never developed appropriate study habits, nor the discipline and patience to sit and listen to a foreign language for eight to ten hours a day.

Although I had achieved a decent grade point average in high school and was considered intelligent, the truth is, my grades had been based primarily on my good behavior and the fact that I was a basketball star who was well-liked by my teachers. Unfortunately, where I came from these attributes were more important than school subjects. When I graduated from high school, the state of South Carolina was ranked #48 in the nation for education.

That did not mean much to me until I met a young lady one Saturday afternoon while in downtown Monterey at Cannery Row. She was tall and attractive, very well-spoken, and extraordinarily articulate. I was impressed and felt a bit smitten.

Trying to be smooth and casual, I asked her, "What's your classification?"

"I don't understand what you're saying," she said.

"You know, are you a junior or a senior in college?" I asked. I figured she was at least an undergrad.

"Uh, I'm in the 10th grade," she said.

I thought, whoa, here I am, an 18-year-old active-duty military man trying to speak with a young girl in the 10th grade. I immediately but politely ended the conversation and began to walk back to the Presidio. It was a short walk up a long, steep hill. As I made the trek, I reflected on the importance of a good education. I had honestly thought I was speaking with someone who was in college. I thought hard about that experience. Why did she speak that way? How did she sound so much older than I thought she was? That is when I realized that the education system in South Carolina was far behind that of California.

Even now, South Carolina's education system continually ranks near the bottom third in the U.S. The state has not made significant reforms since the 1980s—only a shocking 20 percent of African-American eighth graders pass state reading and math tests, compared to 50 percent of white students.[9]

I knew, then and there, that I had to educate myself. I was intelligent, but I had not prioritized my own education. Now I had to learn this foreign language and culture. Beyond that, I had to adapt to a new environment where I was one of three African-American Navy men within the Naval Security Group detachment, and the only one in my Korean class.

I had to work hard and often found myself in moments of self-discovery and reflection. I had just turned 18 years old, and I was clearly among the youngest on the entire military installation. Many of my classmates and Navy colleagues had previously attended college for a time, were college graduates, or prior service members. So, most of them were older and more prepared for the rigors of learning a difficult language such as Korean than I was. I had received Cs in basic English, English II, and Literature in high school. Now I was learning Korean, and it was not easy.

I kept at it—and I even did well. I had an overall passing score, though my listening comprehension was under the established guidelines, which is the most critical part of becoming a linguist. I was still all in at that point and volunteered to take on extended coursework to increase my listening comprehension proficiency.

---

9   According to a report by The Post and Courier, achievement gaps, especially among students of color, remain a huge concern today,https://data.postandcourier.com/saga/minimally-adequate/page/1.

But nearly halfway through the course, I was informed that I had to visit our Navy administrative office to discuss my occupational training plan, which is a formal part of our military service record.

After class that afternoon, I arrived back at the Naval Security Group Detachment's administrative office.

"Hello, Petty Officer Miller, I am Seaman Earl. I am here to review and discuss my occupational training."

"Yes, Seaman Earl. Thank you for coming in today."

Our discussion was about the potential for submarine duty and other navy assignments, also about the possibility of including reconnaissance airplanes, Navy ships, and overseas shore duty in my job as a Korean linguist. Submarine duty is voluntary, and part of the process of applying includes psychological tests, screening for claustrophobia, and other training. I remember being in a total daze, imagining myself on a Navy submarine with headphones on listening to a foreign language, the idea of which was unsettling to say the least. The thought of being on a Navy submarine genuinely concerned me. It would mean spending months and miles under the ocean in listening to and translating communications intercepts in confined spaces with over 130 men. I could not think of anything more challenging for me at that stage in my life. I remembered signing a document, but I was not clear on what I had committed to. However, I do recall immediately losing all motivation and interest in becoming a Korean linguist at that point. Weeks later, I eventually washed out of the course.

Later, my military advisors pushed me into a Spanish language course for about a week and a half. Though I had two years of high school Spanish, I had lost all interest in being a linguist, regardless of what language I was learning. The career counselor asked me to consider becoming an air warfare weatherman on an aircraft carrier or a cryptologic collection technician specializing in Morse code.

Back then, Morse code was used heavily on naval war ships for communicating with their bases and to provide critical information, so the U.S. Navy needed Morse code technicians for detection and collection against adversarial nations. A military instructor facilitated a Morse code test for me where I had to wear headphones and the device started playing these *dot, dot, deedee, dot, dot* sounds. It was very loud and felt painful in my ears, I then ripped the headphones off and threw them to the floor.

"I can't do this," I said.

I discovered early on that I knew what was, and was not, a fit for me. The leadership at the Navy Security Group detachment liked and thought very highly of me, so they then offered cryptologic technician communications training, and I agreed. I was reclassified and issued official military orders to the Naval Technical Training Center, Pensacola, Florida, to be trained as a cryptologic technician (communications).

Although the experience at the Defense Language Institute had been quite the challenge, filled with many highs and lows for an 18-year-old; looking back, I realize this was an important period of self-discovery.[10] I had my eyes opened to other ways of thinking and was able to make the changes I needed to succeed, particularly as they related to the importance of educational excellence, adapting to environmental

---

10   Self-discovery is defined the act or process of achieving self-knowledge. https://www. merriam-webster.com/dictionary/self-discovery

change, and navigating other nationalities and cultures. It was all so different from life on Cherry Street. The most valuable lesson I learned in my Korean class is that failing can be our best lesson. I would not be where I am today had it not been for my experiences.

CHAPTER 4

MISTAKES AND FAILURES

Naval Cryptology—The Signals Intelligence (SIGINT) World

"Mistakes and failures should be options for growth."
—Anonymous

I n the summer of 1982, after eight rigorous months at the Defense Language Institute, I was reclassified and transferred to the Naval Technical Training Center Corry Station in Pensacola, Florida to train as a cryptologist. This was the beginning of my entry into the cryptologic community and signals intelligence (SIGINT)[11] world.

---

11 Signals intelligence (SIGINT) involves collecting foreign intelligence from communications and information systems and providing it to customers across the U.S. Government, such as senior civilian and military officials. They then use the information to help protect U.S. troops, support U.S. allies, fight terrorism, combat international crime and narcotics trades, support diplomatic negotiations, and advance many other important national objectives. https://www.nsa.gov/about/fasigint-faqs/

My three-month training period included special intelligence communications support for air, surface, and shore information processing, using computer terminals. There was technical instruction on communications systems and networks including: satellite systems, modems, routers, security devices, and other cryptographic and state-of-the-art signal analysis equipment.

I was among the top performing sailors in my class. This classroom experience was quite different from my previous one as it was more technical and hands-on, as opposed to the speaking, reading, and writing of the Korean language back in the classrooms at the Defense Language Institute. During this training, I felt much more comfortable with my peer group because many of the other sailors were in my age range.

Pensacola, Fla. (June 4, 2008) The Navy flight demonstration squadron, the "Blue Angels," fly over at the Center for Information Dominance (CID) Corry Station, Pensacola (formerly Naval Technical Training Center (NTTC). U.S. Navy photo by Gary Nichols (Released).

Although being in sunny Florida during the summer months was a lot of fun, one major incident occur that could have ended my fledgling career in the Navy. It was a Thursday night at the base enlisted club, and a couple of friends and I had an altercation with an older sailor from the Naval Air Station nearby. Within a few minutes, the base military police had arrived on the scene. As they jumped out of their vehicles, I recall seeing bright spotlights, blue lights flashing, sirens, and a lot of yelling, "Stop! Stop!" Scared and afraid, we all ran in different directions. I ran towards the barracks, where the electronic warfare students lived and ran up three or four flights of stairs, where I noticed an exit to the rooftop, and I hid there. I remained there for approximately five hours, because the military police, had locked the base down and were using K-9 dogs to search for me and the others. I even saw a helicopter but was not sure if it was part of the manhunt. I have never been so afraid in my life.

When the sun was about to rise at dawn the next day, I prayed to God to guide my path. Still afraid, I left the rooftop and walked towards the main gate where the military police building was located, and turned myself in.

When I walked in, an apparent witness to the altercation, stood up, pointed at me, and yelled, "There he is, that's him!"

Then one of the military police officers, rushed towards me and asked, "Are you Kenneth Earl?"

"Yes, sir, I am," I responded.

The officer explained my rights. And then said to me, "You will be charged under the Uniform Code of Military Justice, with an Article 128, Assault and Battery for the altercation you were involved in. Would you like to make a statement?"

I then stated, "I waive my right to remain silent, and yes, I would like to write a statement of what happened leading up to the alternation, because I didn't start this."

He responded, "Fine," and provided me with a formal personal statement form and a pen. I later learned that I was facing a possibility of a bad conduct discharge, forfeiture of all pay and allowances, and confinement in the Navy Brig for six months.

Given the serious nature of my offense, a Marine Corps gunnery sergeant, who had served in Vietnam, was assigned as my counselor as part of the inquiry process. It turned out to be a blessing for me, and God's answer to my prayer, because he understood my predicament, believed in me, and assisted in my representation in a case of self-defense.

With his raspy, drill sergeant voice, he said, "Sailor, tell me what happened."

I described the entire series of events that led up to the night in question. "Gunny, the guy I allegedly assaulted, had placed a firearm in my face and threatened me the previous week, and there were witnesses. And on that day, we all got into a shouting match inside the enlisted club parking lot, and we followed him. He then reached into the trunk of his car and pulled out a handgun and pointed it at me. I blacked out and all I remembered after that was all of us hiding behind the side of a building."

The gunnery sergeant asked, "Did you or the others report this incident?"

"No Gunny, I didn't report, and I don't think any of the others did," I said.

"Why not?" he asked.

I shared with him I that was afraid to tell the authorities and was simply happy to get out of the situation with my life. I told him that when I saw the individual on base the following week, I was afraid that he would follow through on his threat, and I did initiate that altercation. Moments later, the military police arrived on the scene with sirens blaring and lights flashing. Fearing the cops, and uncertain of what to do, I ran and hid on top of the building and stayed there for hours, alone and afraid.

I told the gunnery sergeant that I had learned and understood that *two wrongs do not make a right,* and that that was something my mother had instilled in me from a young age. However, she had also said, "If someone hits you, hit them back," which may be a total contradiction, but I understood she was telling me to stand up for myself.

"But in this situation, I was afraid. This guy had threatened my life and I felt I had no other alternative," I said.

The gunnery sergeant told me he understood because he had served in the warzone of Vietnam and had faced life or death situations, but he did admonish me.

"You can't take the law into your own hands," he said. "That's the mistake you made here. You should have reported this incident because other sailors were at risk as well."

He told me he would give the additional information to the investigating officials for their review and consideration.

After the investigation into the incident was completed, the investigators discovered that the individual was not from the base and did have a firearm, but he claimed he had not threatened me. The investigation found that there were too many conflicting statements by witnesses on both sides to proceed with a court-martial, and the case against me was dropped and then dismissed at the Executive Officer (XO) inquiry level, with no charges and no documentation placed on the record. The XO inquiry was a very formal process. I recall standing at attention and parade rest throughout. The gunnery sergeant and my instructor both spoke on my behalf.

"Commander, sir, I have had the opportunity to get to know Seaman Earl these last several weeks. He understands the mistakes he has made with regard to this incident, and he takes full responsibility for his actions. I believe he is a good sailor, and I recommend no further disciplinary actions," said the gunnery sergeant.

My instructor then followed, saying, "Seaman Earl is among the top students in my training course, he respects the chain of command, and he has taken responsibility and accountability for his actions. With the exception of this incident, he has been a model sailor and I recommend no further disciplinary action."

The XO did not hold back, and he laid into me with a stern warning. "I better not ever see you again; if I even see you walking on the base, you're out of my Navy! Hell, if I even hear your name again," he yelled, "you're out of my Navy! You hear me, Seaman Earl?!"

I said, "Aye-aye, sir, aye-aye, sir!"

"You are free to go."

This was the most terrifying experience of my life, on multiple levels. Firstly, I did not want to receive a bad conduct or dishonorable discharge and be sent home back to South Carolina. Secondly—and even more importantly—I did not want to disappoint my mother. Even until this day, though, I cannot remember the gunnery sergeant's name. I believe that he not only saved many of his comrades in Vietnam, but he also saved me, my military career, and the future of an 18-year-old kid from Cherry Street. I thanked God for sending me a guardian angel through that process, and I made a promise to never put myself in a situation like that ever again.

So, I remained among the top sailors in my graduating class. In October 1982, I received military orders to Pearl Harbor, Hawaii, to serve on the flag staff of the Commander, Submarine Force, U.S. Pacific Fleet.

CHAPTER 5

OVERCOMING FEAR

Commander, Submarine Force, U.S. Pacific
Fleet, Pearl Harbor, Hawaii

*"He who is not every day conquering some fear has not learned the
secret of life."*

—Ralph Waldo Emerson

November 1982, my airplane had just landed at Honolulu International Airport on the island of Oahu. Dressed in my Navy summer whites uniform, I was met by my Navy sponsor and his wife. He handed me a Hawaiian lei to welcome me to the island. Immediately, I knew I was in paradise. Everywhere I looked it seemed I was surrounded by beautiful palm trees, crystal-clear blue waters, and bright, warm sunlight.

Commander, Submarine Force, U.S. Pacific Fleet (COMSUB-PAC), Pearl Harbor, Hawaii was my first permanent duty station. Our overall mission was to provide logistical support, manpower, and operational plans to maintain the ability of the submarine force in the Pacific Area of Responsibility (AOR) to deliver anti-submarine warfare, anti-surface ship warfare, precision land strike, mine warfare, intelligence, surveillance and early warning, and special warfare and strategic deterrence capabilities.[12] In support of this important mission, I worked as a submarine broadcast operator within the Special Intelligence Communications (SPINTCOMM) division.

The Virginia-class submarine USS Texas departs the Joint Base Pearl Harbor-Hickam. June 23, 2011, in Pearl Harbor, Hawaii. Photo by MCS2 Ronald Gutridge/US Navy via Planetpix.

Working in special intelligence communications to support national missions was fascinating and exciting. But it was also scary and high risk from a national security, diplomatic, and political perspective. Much of my work involved special access programs (SAPs). SAPs are highly classified programs designed to protect the planning, execution, and support of sensitive military activi-

---

12 Commander, Submarine Pacific https://www.csp.navy.mil/About-SUBPAC/.

ties. Because of the nature of our operations, I cannot discuss the details in this book. Nonetheless, it was a very chilling experience for a 19-year-old kid from Cherry Street to find myself suddenly supporting the front lines where U.S. national security was at stake and lives were at risk.

I performed shift work, where I worked a 2–2–96 schedule, meaning we worked two 12-hour days, 24 hours off, then two 12-hour nights, then 96 hours, or four days, off. This was a great work schedule, especially if you were living in Hawaii. Sports were huge on the island and intra-service rivalries between the Army, Air Force, Navy and Marines were fierce and highly competitive. I spent most of my four days off playing sports, specifically basketball and flag football. I also took a few college courses at Hawaii Pacific University.

During my free time, I had a part-time job at a liquor store, "Wine and Spirits," at the Salt Lake Shopping Center. I enjoyed interacting with the customers and developed connections with the store regulars. Given that Oahu has 125 beaches and that the entire island is only 44 miles long and 30 miles across, and that Wine and Spirits was centrally located, I guess it is not surprising that one of the top selling products was the Budweiser 12-packs.

Though I worked for a liquor store, I could not purchase alcohol due to being 19 years old, while the legal age was 21. However, the submarine base allowed sailors who were 18 and older to purchase beer, but in the base club only.

After having lived in the Navy barracks for about five months, I moved off-base into a studio apartment in the Salt Lake neighborhood only three blocks from the Wine and Spirits. It was a three-and-a-half-mile bike ride from the submarine base at Pearl Harbor, which helped me stay in shape. This was my first time living on my own and paying rent.

My studio was on the third level of a garden-style apartment complex. The apartments did not have individual washers and dryers, but instead had a central laundromat. In fact, one time, someone actually stole my clothes from the laundromat, and I could not believe it—*who does that?* A few days later and much to my shock, I ran into a guy we called "Juice" (from New York), wearing my Navy shirt and khaki pants! I could not believe my eyes. Let us just say that I handled the matter, and it was unlikely "Juice" would ever as much as touch my clothes again.

My tour of duty at COMSUBPAC would be two years. The work I undertook was considered vital to national security and of serious consequence. We worked in a highly secured sensitive compartmented information facility (SCIF) located in the basement of a relatively small building complex about 50 yards from where the submarines docked.

Most days, operations and conditions were normal. But one night, about two hours into my 12-hour shift, there was an alert involving our special mission operations.

We had to abandon our normal procedures and move to emergency operations and response. This was not an exercise, and our actions were critical—it was a real-world crisis situation involving special mission operations, intelligence, and surveillance.

As the submarine broadcast operator, I specialized in many cryptographic systems. On this particular night, I was working on our

Special Intelligence Submarine Satellite Information Exchange Subsystem (SSIXS) when I received the alert.

I immediately yelled out to my supervisor, "Rick, we have an alert." He and the technical controller hurried over to my position and observed it.

Everything stopped and my supervisor directed me to, "Break the scheduled broadcast now and prepare the notifications."

He then instructed another team member to "Go to the operations center and advise the command duty officer (CDO) that we have an alert, and that his attention is needed URGENTLY."

Minutes later, the CDO arrived, and my supervisor briefed him that this matter was critical. The CDO stated, "I have to inform the chief of staff and the admiral. I will be right back."

Our team spent the next seven hours coordinating, reporting, and providing vital communications in response to the crisis situation. Due to the gravely sensitive and classified nature of the operation and the event, I cannot disclose any specifics, but it is safe to say that the mission was eventually secured, and our response was of critical importance.

When we returned to all conditions normal, it suddenly dawned on me what my job was really about and how special intelligence operations and cryptology play a pivotal role in the security of our nation.

That seven-hour period was all the education, experience, and clarity I needed to understand what national security was and why our communications and secrets require protection. I realized I could not afford to make any mistakes, and what I was involved with could not be discussed outside the classified and secured space I worked in. All the special access program paperwork I had read and signed, and the oath I had taken before this incident, now all made sense.

The remainder of our shift was quiet. Even though I was the youngest and least experienced on the team, I could see and feel the calm, quiet and relief, as well as the mental exhaustion of my supervisor and other team members. When the shift ended at about 6:45 a.m., I rolled my bicycle through the building to the front exit. When I stepped outside, I looked straight ahead, and I was so filled with fear and anxiety, I did not know which direction I would take.

I was confused and scared, convinced that I would be followed or be under surveillance. I normally went to the left, but as I rode off to the right, thoughts flooded my mind. *Am I being watched? Is someone trailing me?* It hit me that I was carrying out highly classified work and if I were to make a mistake or discuss the work we were doing, I could cause an international incident, conflict or even a war. I was shaken to the core.

After that, outside of work, I isolated for quite a while, not interacting with my friends, and I even stopped working at Wine and Spirits to give myself more personal time and mental space. It was overwhelming and I had this intense, persistent worry because of the stress of the event and the fear of making a mistake in the future. At 19 years old, that night changed me and my perspectives about this important work we were supporting for the nation.

To overcome the fear and anxiety, I dedicated my free time to learning more about the cryptologic community and my craft. I developed competencies and became more proficient and professional at the job duties and responsibilities. My mindset began to shift, and my confidence rose. That fear made me focus harder. I turned that fear into something productive and made it work for me. That is when I became really good at my job. I studied hard and learned all I could about submarine operations, cryptographic systems, and telecommunications. I think the quote by Ralph Waldo Emerson I mentioned at the start of the chapter sums this up nicely.

I began to receive accolades from senior leadership, and recognition from performing as a top submarine broadcast operator. Two years prior, I had been having difficulty with learning a foreign language and had been hiding from the military police on the roof of a building. Now, I was at the top of my game as a submarine broadcast operator. With fewer than four years of naval service, I was promoted to petty officer second class (E-5).

CHAPTER 6

PERSEVERANCE

USS Blue Ridge (LCC-19) Yokosuka, Japan

Definition: *Perseverance is a continued effort to do or achieve something despite difficulties, failure, or opposition.*[13]

It was July 1985. I took an exceptionally long 13-hour, 6,200-mile transpacific flight, from Chicago, Illinois to the Narita International Airport in Tokyo, Japan. When I stepped off the large 747 aircraft that contained more than 500-plus passengers, I realized I had never been anywhere more foreign. As I walked through the airport, I had difficulty understanding the signage, so I found myself just following the other passengers to the customs section. I do not recall seeing any other American passengers on that flight.

---

13 Perseverance is defined as the continued effort to do or achieve something despite difficulties, failure, or opposition. https://www.merriam-webster.com/dictionary/perseverance

Shimizu, Japan (May 30, 2008). The amphibious command ship USS Blue Ridge (LCC-19) steams within sight of Mt. Fuji on its final stop to Shimizu, ending a six-week Spring Swing tour. Blue Ridge serves under Commander, Expeditionary Strike Group (ESG) 7/Task Force (CTF) 76, the Navy's only forward deployed amphibious force. U.S. Navy.

I was finally able to make it through the maze of this seemingly very large airport to an awaiting military bus heading towards Yokosuka Naval Station, which was a two-hour trip away. When the bus arrived in Yokosuka, I was directed to the Navy barracks on base because my ship, the USS Blue Ridge (LCC-19) was deployed out to sea on a Western Pacific deployment. I was assigned to work temporarily at Commander, U.S. Naval Forces, Japan (CNFJ), the headquarters building near the main gate, for about five or six weeks while I awaited the return of my ship. During that time, I was introduced to Samuel Butler. Samuel was a petty officer first class (E-6) and the special intelligence communications supervisor at CNFJ Headquarters. I recall he had the letter "V" on his Navy achievement medal ribbon, which denoted heroism or valor in combat, an honor all sailors recognized and respected because it was rare. Sam was a great guy, universally liked and admired by everyone. He had these wide, black-framed eyeglasses called Gazelles, and I recall he enjoyed his occasional Johnnie Walker Red

Label blended scotch whisky. He and his wife took particularly good care of me, both while at work and off duty, because living in this environment was literally foreign to me and to all who were stationed there for the first time. I lived in the barracks on the relatively large naval base, and I would walk to work or catch a taxi.

One day Sam asked, "Kenneth, would you like to use our car to get around?"

I said, "I don't have a driver's license."

Appearing surprised, he asked, "How old are you?"

"I'm 21, but the reason I don't have a driver's license is a long story going back to elementary school when I wrecked my mother's car."

He laughed, and said, "It doesn't matter, Kenneth. You would need an international driver's license here in Japan anyway." They then taught me how to drive and parallel park—it must be noted that the driver's side of a vehicle in Japan is the opposite to American auto standards. I did obtain my international driver's license, and eventually received my U.S. driver's license at age 24, when I had returned to the U.S.

As soon as the Blue Ridge arrived back in port, it would mark the start of my first duty assignment aboard a U.S. Navy ship, and I was nervous and apprehensive. I called my older brother who was still on active duty in the Air Force at the time. I looked up to him and knew I could trust his judgment, and that he would provide the encouragement and motivation I was seeking.

"Preston," I said. "I am a bit uneasy about going on this ship, for some reason. This is totally different than anything I have experienced up to this point in my career, and I just have an instinct that it's going to be outside my comfort zone."

"Just do your thing. Of course, it *is* different, but you will be fine," he told me. "I believe in you, and I know you can do it."

That was all I needed. "Great," I said. "I will keep you posted."

I wanted to prove him right, and when the ship returned, I boarded the ship and was met on the quarterdeck by my Navy sponsor, Christopher Welch. My previous duty station had been a highly professional submarine command staff, but my first impression upon entry into my new workspace was not good and not quite the same as my previous command. Though my sponsor was polite and squared away, the work area was somewhat in disarray and the few sailors I met initially were not welcoming and seemed to dismiss my presence.

We worked in a secured, classified area of the ship called the Ships Signals Exploitation Space. The space was equipped with cryptologic tools, capabilities, and gear designed to perform real-time signals intelligence analysis, and the functions necessary to acquire, identify, locate, and track communications, voice, and electronic signals. My primary role was to provide special tactical intelligence communications and cryptographic support to the operational mission.

The ship's complement or number of crew members and command staff was approximately 260 officers and 1,173 enlisted men. Though I served onboard the USS Blue Ridge, I was assigned to the Commander, Seventh Fleet Staff, headed by a three-star admiral, so my official duty station was the Commander, Seventh Fleet that was embarked on the USS Blue Ridge. The staff and crew had separate chains of command and each culture could not have been more different.

Our cryptologic division was relatively small, made up of about 20 personnel, and a large portion of the division consisted of special intelligence communications technicians. Although this was my area of expertise and excellence, I was only one of two African Americans on the team.

Though adjusting and trying to fit in with the 20 members of our cryptologic division was quite the challenge by itself, living in a closely confined forward-berthing area with 80 men was even more difficult. The range of personalities, backgrounds, and behaviors spanned the entire spectrum. On some days, the culture of the ship's crew looked and felt like scenes from a federal prison, the *Escape From New York* movie, and the *Survivor Island* series all combined. All the main action took place on the mess deck. The mess deck is the large area of the ship were the enlisted crew members gathered, primarily to eat and socialize. Card games, chess, and especially dominos were popular activities onboard the USS Blue Ridge. With more than 1,000 enlisted crew members, cliques were formed and there would be the occasional altercation or disagreement among the crew. A lot of yelling, bragging, and chaos arose from time to time.

Even the most mundane things could be a challenge. I recall one incident during mid-rats. Mid-rats were dinner leftovers served around midnight to those sailors working from 8 p.m. to 12 midnight and from 12 midnight to 4 a.m.

There are four meals a day onboard ship: breakfast, lunch, dinner, and mid-rats. It was about 11:45 p.m., and I was the only customer in the mess hall serving line. The Navy mess specialist (chef) on the other side of the serving line placed a slice of meatloaf, a scoop of mashed potatoes and gravy, and about four or five green beans on my tray. In silence, he placed the tray on the top shelf of the serving line. I asked if he could give me more green beans.

"What?" he asked.

"Can I have more green beans?" I repeated.

"No, you cannot," he said.

"Why not?"

"Because I said so."

"You act as if you own this place, and these are your green beans."

He was a big guy, and he came out from behind the serving line, with his apron and chef hat on and his dukes up, squaring off and ready to fight. It was a crazy scene to say the least, and well-illustrated the tension that lies below the surface when everyone lives in such close quarters.

It was not unusual for some individuals to try to size you up. A common refrain was. "Where you from?" It sometimes felt like they were trying to determine your affiliation of something, but generally, it was a way of initiating communication, a way to get to know you and to determine whether they could trust you.

Because I conducted myself professionally, and I worked in a classified work area, some of the Blue Ridge crew members suspected that I was a narc, a federal agent. There were several drug-related investigations ongoing when I arrived on the ship and many of the crew thought that I was part of the Office of Naval Criminal Investigations (NCIS) team, assigned to those cases while undercover.

It was both a good and bad thing for me. The good part was that no one would bother me, but the bad was that they did not necessarily trust me and were always on guard or suspicious of my presence. Yes, I did classified work for the staff, but I was not a narc. Those perceptions made it difficult for me to have close interactions or personal relationships with many in my peer group.

I spent two years living onboard ship, and whether at sea or in port, the forward berthing was my home as I did not qualify for the pay and allowances needed to support living off the ship. My rack (bed), the lockers, shower, and restrooms were all in a very confined area. A married sailor, regardless of paygrade, could live off the ship. However, living off-base in Japan is expensive even with the additional pay and allowances. During those times, the Blue Ridge was not outfitted to support women who were permanently assigned onboard the ship. This policy has since changed.

Enlisted Berthing Area - USS Midway CV-41.

Ship life was difficult for me from many perspectives. Not only did I have to live on the ship full time, but I also suffered from the worst sea sickness. The Blue Ridge was a relatively large ship and when the seas were high and rough, I would become terribly sick. It would be so bad I would have to leave my workstation to go lay down. The ship's corpsman would prescribe Dramamine for the nausea and dizziness, which was not always 100 percent effective. As a side note, and to show you how small this world is, the corpsman that provided me with the Dramamine over 35 years ago currently works in my division and current place of employment as a cybersecurity engineer. He too retired from the U.S. Navy some time ago as a master chief petty officer (E-9).

During down times and while in port, I would typically spend time with my girlfriend, who lived in Yokohama. I would also hang out on the Honch, which was a strip of craft shops, bars, and restaurants in Yokosuka, or in Tokyo. Tokyo was a bit like New York City—the music, the food, the big city lights, and the shows—but there is really nothing like Tokyo, Japan. Japanese culture is the best. The Japanese people work hard and play hard, and Japan has one of the most courteous and respectful societies I have ever encountered.

Our ship made multiple deployments to the Western Pacific, including to countries such as the Philippines, Hong Kong, Australia, Singapore, and South Korea.

Basketball was huge on the Blue Ridge and our team was one of the best military teams in Japan. And yes, of course, I was on the team. I have many positive memories of winning games and tournaments and my best relationships and friends were members of the Blue Ridge's basketball team. But my most memorable experience was when we made a port visit to Cebu. Cebu is a small Philippine island south of the capital of Manila, and at the time was among the poorest islands in the Philippines. Our port visit there was for humanitarian and diplomatic purposes. The Navy called it *showing the flag.* The planners of the visit scheduled a basketball exhibition game for charity. Many of the island people showed up and it was as if our team was the Harlem Globetrotters. Dressed in our basketball uniforms, the people there made us feel proud. It was obvious they did not have any material wealth, but they were so happy to see us. They loved us and showed affection and admiration. I felt on top of the world.

Cebu City, Philippines, 11.March 2012: Filipino kids having fun during a downpour as the raining season comes to an end.

I recall this one little kid—he could not have been more than eight years old. "Hello mister," he said.

I responded, "Hi there, what's your name?"

He said, "My name is Ramil, can I touch your hair?"

I leaned down and said, "Sure."

He rubbed my head and so did his friend. They seemed amazed. "You are tall," they said.

Neither he nor his little friends had shoes on their feet. They surrounded me and a couple of my fellow basketball players in pure joy. It just felt so warm, real, and unconditional. Those moments were worth all the trials and challenges I had faced. This encounter demonstrated real humanity to me, and it took me back to life on Cherry Street. It made me think of what my mother may have experienced in her youth and the challenges she faced during the Jim Crow era in the segregated south, where opportunities where limited or non-existent.

When I reflect on my time and life in the military, this visit to Cebu stands out the most as it made me ponder deeply on my own life. It really touched me. These people did not have much of anything, but they had each other, and they understood the meaning of joy and happiness. Even though it was a small and simple facility, it was full of families enjoying us playing a basketball game. They were cheering with excitement and even amazement. I had played basketball around the world, including a high-profile game against a Chinese national team in Hong Kong, but nothing like the experience in Cebu!

Back onboard the ship, I had some challenges within my division. I worked hard to fit in and be one of the guys, but it did not always happen. However, despite my initial disappointment, I continued to be friendly and cordial. I even went so far as to wear a cowboy hat and boots and went out to local country bars with the guys in my division just to blend in, even though that is not my thing at all. Sadly, it did not work or help the situation along.

At the time, I recognized it as a clique thing and that there was a new-guy trust factor at play.

I had a real awakening when I received my first performance appraisal. The rating surprised me—my individual performance scores and overall rating were much lower than I had anticipated, especially given I was among the top performers in that I was technically proficient and extraordinarily professional among the sailors within the division.

I asked my supervisor, "Why is my rating so low?" My peers had already shared their outstanding ratings with me ahead of my session, and they all were excited. His response was shocking and was among the most blatant displays of intolerance I had ever experienced professionally at that point in my career and life for that matter.

With a change of voice and tone, he said, "You know, when you talk, you talk with your hands, you know, like you be jive talking." I sat there stunned, but he went even further. He stood up and said, "You know, this is how you be walking," and he started moving his hands and walking as he was imitating my style of walking.

He flat-out mocked me, strongly defending his assessment and justification for my lower marks. He then sat back down.

I looked at him and said, "Oh, okay, I see what's happening here, I get it."

In that moment, I recognized and learned that from that point forward, I needed to stop trying to fit in and being one of the guys, because that would never be possible. It was clear that my supervisor had, without question, stereotyped me, and I certainly did not find it amusing. It bordered on straight ignorance and racial bias. I later learned that he and a core group of his buddies had been concealing and covering up for one another's inappropriate behavior and activities during our four-mouth deployment and for periods of time before my arrival.

Despite his lack of appropriateness and his unfortunate behavior, I do credit him for teaching me a valuable lesson of the importance of just being myself. No matter what we do in life, no one can beat you at being you. And from that time on, I stopped trying to fit in and be one of the guys, and someone I was not.

Even though I experienced those moments of adversity, I persevered and overcame all the challenges and resistance from nearly every angle. I kept going, kept pushing, and in the end it all made me stronger!

After two years in Hawaii and two years in Japan, I was ready to head back to the east coast with an entirely different perspective on who I was. I then received official orders to go to Washington, D.C.

CHAPTER 7

DEFEATING AND OVERCOMING MYSELF

Naval Security Station - 3801 Nebraska Avenue,
Washington D.C.

"My biggest problem in life was overcoming myself. But once I defeated
myself, the only thing left was peace..."

—Kevin Gates

I n July 1987, I reported to the Naval Security Station (NAVSEC-
STA), 3801 Nebraska Avenue, in Washington, D.C. The Naval
Security Station was home to the Commander, Naval Security Group
Command headquarters, which was responsible for cryptology and
signals intelligence for naval forces operating world-wide.

I performed an array of duties and responsibilities, including communications watch supervisor, training coordinator, and systems
and network manager. I also played a major role in the establish-
ment of the first secured classified intelligence network between

the Naval Security Group and the National Security Agency that provided high-speed connectivity and special messaging. Additionally, one of the main duties I had was as an operations manager for the communications system that provided classified messages and intelligence products to a variety of system users and Commander, Naval Security Group customers.

Formerly the Naval Security Station located at 3801 Nebraska Avenue Washington D.C., now the Headquarters for the U.S. Department of Homeland Security (DHS).

The Naval Security Group Command was later relocated and eventually aligned under the Naval Network Warfare Command at U.S. Fleet Cyber Command. This group is responsible for the Navy's information network operations, offensive and defensive cyber operations, space operations and signals intelligence as the naval component of the U.S. Cyber Command at Fort George G. Meade, Maryland, home to the National Security Agency (NSA). 3801 Nebraska Avenue is now the headquarters for the U.S. Department of Homeland Security.

NAVSECSTA was my first permanent duty station in the continental U.S., just 478 miles and a seven-hour drive away from my home in Columbia, South Carolina. After six years away, I was happy to be back home in the States and to be close to my family and friends. But when I arrived, D.C. was not what I had envisioned. I had imagined peace, liberty, and happiness in the Nation's capital. In fact, in 1987, D.C. was known as the murder capital of the U.S.[14] There were 225 murders the year I arrived, and that had eventually increased to 472 murders the year I departed—it was a dangerous city back then. Though I was glad to be home, this was not the country I had known when I had departed for the Navy, nor did my new life and lifestyle compared to how I had been living overseas in Hawaii and Japan.

One night, I was out with a couple of Navy friends celebrating a birthday and we missed witnessing a drive-by shooting by just a few minutes. Someone had shot a young African-American male three times—and we saw him lying on the ground right after it happened. Some people began to run from the scene, where my friends and I were standing in shock looking at the young man lying there dead, killed instantly. The D.C. Metropolitan Police and news trucks soon arrived on the scene. Police tape was rolled out and the crowd started to grow.

This was at the height of the drug crisis in D.C. It was like a war zone. I never saw anything like that in Hawaii or Japan. In fact, I had come home to a major drug epidemic in the United States. Not only was it bad in D.C., but it had also impacted my hometown of Columbia.

---

14 District of Columbia Crime Rates: http://www.disastercenter.com/crime/dccrime. htm.

As a kid, I never experienced that sort of destruction and lack of care in the communities where I grew up. I do recall that when I was in the seventh grade, two of my friends and I discovered an older guy who lived in the neighborhood who had apparently overdosed on what appeared to be heroin. We had been walking to the neighborhood park to play basketball when we saw him. He was frozen in a seated position, not breathing, or moving. It seemed he had been dead for a while. We saw the needle that was still in his arm, the spoon, and what looked like a drug kit nearby. Scared and shaken, we ran to the nearest home and knocked on the door and told an elderly man what we had found. He called the Richland County Sheriff Office. It was the most terrifying thing I had ever seen until I saw the man who was shot in D.C.

On some level, I understood how it could have happened. I knew that life could have been different for me had I made different choices. There were not many opportunities for the people in my neighborhood. Unemployment levels were high—especially if you were young and did not have a good education or a trade. Upon reflection, had I not decided to join the Navy, I could have easily fallen prey to what had, in the time I had been away, become a very widespread problem affecting many families and good people.

Neighborhoods were devastated by the lack of economic development, few good paying job opportunities, and the sale of highly addictive crack cocaine in poor communities. Peddlers of the drug and users were being arrested in alarming numbers, thereby impacting entire communities. That could have been my story, but I credit my mother for encouraging me to do positive things with my life. I recall my mother telling me around age of 15 or 16 that as a growing man, I needed to find my way and be on my own once I graduated from high school, and not to remain under her roof. It may have felt a bit harsh at the time, but she was just pushing me out of the nest and driving me to make something of my life.

Upon my return to the States and having observed the conditions of my home neighborhood, I knew I needed to keep my distance from some of my old classmates who had been affected by the drug epidemic in my hometown. I also knew I needed to reflect on and take charge of my thoughts, emotions and spirituality and make some deliberate decisions about my social and professional life. I was now a Naval cryptologist trusted with national security secrets. Not that I was better than anyone else, but I needed to continue to grow as a man and a professional and make my mother and family proud.

Though Columbia was my home, it was time to leave the past behind. I was no longer in high school, but a young man. I was 23 at the time. I knew I needed to build on the lessons I had learned over the past few years, and to continue to improve as a professional and as a human being. I particularly needed to work on how I handled adversity, conflict, and differences with others. Understanding that I needed to change, I started to study and incorporate the principles of emotional intelligence into my daily life.[15]

I overcame and defeated myself—that kid who did not manage emotions well and hid on roof tops—by focusing on self-aware-

---

15 What is Emotional Intelligence? Emotional intelligence (otherwise known as emotional quotient or EQ) is the ability to understand, use, and manage your own emotions in positive ways to relieve stress, communicate effectively, empathize with others, overcome challenges, and defuse conflict. Emotional intelligence is commonly defined by four attributes: Self-management; Self-awareness; Social awareness; and Relationship management. https://www.helpguide.org/articles/mental-health/emotional-intelligence-eq.htm

ness, self-management, social awareness, and empathy for others. I committed to change. I became a supervisor, responsible for other personnel. I focused on being a professional and a better version of myself. I knew I was changing when my friends and family told me they noticed the discipline I had developed and that I was carrying myself differently. I knew I was headed down the right path.

Also, I fell in love. I remember it like yesterday. Our buzzer for the classified message center had rung. I went to the window, which was protected by curtains, opened them, and there she was, a beautiful, tall young lady who was also in the Navy and worked as a cryptologic technician administrator. She was there to deliver highly sensitive and classified material as part of her normal routine and duties. I later saw her walking in the parking a lot towards her red Toyota Corolla. That night, I wrote her a letter and signed it "Secret Admirer." A few days later, I placed the letter on driver's side window of her car. The next time I saw her at the message center window, she asked me, "Did you leave a note on my car?"

I responded, "Yes, I did."

Well, three dates later, we were a couple. She had a daughter from a previous marriage, and we became a family, the three of us, and we would spend a total of nine years together over both our Navy careers. Personal growth aside, I was making progress in my professional life as well. I was enjoying my new role as a supervisor and was now in charge of leading and guiding other young men and women and I took that job very seriously.

This, combined with other significant accomplishments, I was promoted to petty officer first class (E6).

Pictured here with my mother in 1990, I was selected as the Naval Security Station Sailor of the Year. My mother received an award for her support and dedication to my naval career. My mother and sister travelled to Washington D.C. for the ceremony, just as they had nine years earlier when they attended my graduation from recruit training "bootcamp" in Orlando, Florida.

My mother receiving a Letter of Appreciation for supporting me throughout my naval career and selection as the Naval Security Station 1990 Sailor of the Year (SOY).

"Kenneth, I'm so proud of you, you have really matured into the man and person I knew you could become," she said.

I responded, "Mom, I thank you for all the life lessons and wisdom you have shared."

"Like all my children, I prayed for you to have a life of accomplishment and fulfilment, but you're still my baby," she said. Everyone laughed when she said that and, let me tell you, it always embarrassed me when she called me her baby in the presence of others.

My division officer presented my mother with the award, and she was so happy that she was brought to tears because it was a surprise she had not anticipated. She displayed that award in her living room with a sense of pride. I owe my naval service and life to my mother, and quite frankly, she deserved even more given the sacrifices she made for me and my siblings, and challenges she faced in her own life.

I subsequently competed for the Sailor of the Year for the entire Navy. Although I did not win, just competing at that level was an honor. As I looked around at the reception for the candidates onboard the USS Barry, a museum ship at the Navy Yard in Washington, D.C., I was blown away that I was even standing there with all the other contenders—let alone the chief of naval operations and the master chief of the navy.

Despite all the trials, failures, and even fear I experienced in my nearly nine years of service, I had competed to be the top, number one sailor for the entire United States Navy. Even today, as I write this book, I wonder how it all happened and I realized I had defeated and overcome myself. And I was now one step closer to cracking the code of life and being the best version of myself.

Reenlistment ceremony, Naval Security Station, 1998

CHAPTER 8

CONFIDENCE

USS Chosin (CG-65) Pearl Harbor, Hawaii

Definition: *Confidence is a feeling or consciousness of one's power or of reliance on one's circumstances.*[16]

In June 1991, I left the Naval Security Station in Washington D.C. to report for the Pre-Commissioning Unit Chosin in Pascagoula, Mississippi. It would be my second permanent assignment on a U.S. Naval ship, a guided-missile cruiser, named in honor of the Battle of Chosin Reservoir during the Korean War.

After several months of pre-commissioning preparations and training in San Diego, California, and visiting my mother, I drove alone from Columbia, South Carolina through Georgia, Alabama,

---

16 Confidence is a feeling or consciousness of one's power or of reliance on one's circumstances https://www.merriam-webster.com/dictionary/confidence

and Mississippi, the Deep South. I recall after passing through Montgomery, Alabama at about 1:30 a.m., headed south towards Pascagoula, Mississippi, I found myself driving along extensive stretches of dark two-lane roads, along miles of which there were no streetlights or even moonlight. No buildings, no people, or even other cars on the road, just stretches of fields, trees, and dark nothingness for what seemed like hours. I began to grow nervous, reflective, and fearful.

Pearl Harbor, Hawaii (Jun. 19, 2002)—USS Chosin (CG-65) makes her return to sea after an extensive eight-month yard period. U.S. Navy photo by Photographer's Mate 1st Class William R. Goodwin.

I feared something was wrong and that something bad was about to happen to me. My senses were on high alert, and I prayed I would not run out of gas or get a flat tire. GPS was not available back then, and I was not sure I was on the right road or even that I was going in the right direction. This was the Deep South that had a terrible history of lynching, assassinations of civil rights activists, church bombings and intense racial unrest.

As a young African-American man, I did not want to break down on the side of the road, or even get pulled over by the highway patrol or local police, so I intentionally drove at or below the speed limit. It seemed like a long, intense dream playing out in my mind as I thought of the history of slavery, segregation, and discrimination in this part of the country and what that meant for me being alone on this dark, two-lane road.

I began to have flashbacks and memories of the summer of July 1982, when I had been visiting family and friends during the Independence Day holiday while on military leave in transit to the Navy Technical Training Center in Pensacola, Florida. I was 18 years old and riding in a car with my high school friend, S.G. S.G. was driving us in his car when we were pulled over on what was suspicion of an expired license plate on North Main Street near I-20 in Columbia. The state trooper engaged with my friend, asking for his license and registration. The trooper noticed an open beer container in the center console. It just happened to be there, although we were not drinking while driving. He asked SG to step out of the car. Looking out of the back window, I observed him conducting a field sobriety test and then I could hear them talking.

The trooper then came to my side of the car and politely asked, "What's your name?"

"Kenneth Earl," I said.

He then opened the door, and said, "Please come with me, let's talk." I walked back with the trooper and he directed me to the passenger seat of the police car. S.G. was still standing at the rear of the car, just looking.

We sat in the car and he explained, "S.G. has expired tags and an open container in the car, but he did pass the sobriety test."

I replied, "That's right, we have not been drinking."

He explained, "But the open container of beer carries a fine." He then asked me, "Do you have any money?" I showed him I had three $20.00 dollar bills. He actually took the $60.00 dollars and said, "I will let you both go."

I then told him, "Sir, that's all I have, and I am in the Navy headed to Florida and need to catch a plane tomorrow morning."

He said, "Show me your military ID." When I did, he looked at me and gave me back $20.00. But that state trooper had literally robbed me. He asked me to step back out and then let my friend and me drive off. He trailed us for a bit, then made a sharp U-turn and headed back towards the I-20. This memory further fueled my anxiety on this awfully long, dark road. I was afraid.

Thoughts of the murder of Emmett Till entered my mind. Emmett Till was born in Chicago and grew up in a middle-class Black neighborhood. He was visiting relatives in Money, Mississippi, in 1955, when the fourteen-year-old was accused of whistling at Carolyn Bryant, a white woman who was a cashier at a grocery store. Four days later, Bryant's husband Roy and his half-brother J.W. Milam kidnapped Till, beat him, and shot him in the head. The men were tried for murder, but an all-white, male jury acquitted them.[17] Thankfully, eventually the sun finally rose and there was light, the fear was gone, and I was back to my normal state of mind. Eventually, I made it to Pascagoula without incident.

---

17 **Emmett Till**. https://www.biography.com/crime-figure/emmett-till

In Pascagoula, I would become a plank owner of the Chosin. Being a plank owner is a special rite of passage in the Navy. Most Navy ships are older and have developed their own reputations and histories over the years. But when you are a plank owner, you are part of the initial crew. You help equip the ship, birth it, and establish the future reputation of the ship's name. Veterans of the Korean War attended our commissioning ceremony in honor of their heroism and sacrifice.

I was instrumental in the coordination and installation of the computer and electronic equipment. I established standard procedures and documentation for operating special intelligence communications systems and provided support for signals intelligence collection and intercept capabilities. We built the ship's signals exploitation space from the ground up, and we took a lot of pride in our accomplishments.

After months of training and outfitting, we departed Ingalls Shipbuilding Shipyard, Pascagoula, Mississippi and headed toward Pearl Harbor for our maiden voyage. To get to Pearl Harbor, we had to travel through the Gulf of Mexico to the Panama Canal. Without the canal, our 27-day transit to Hawaii would have taken triple the amount of time to complete (i.e., 80 days instead of 27 days). The building of the Panama Canal began in 1881 and was completed in 1914. It was designed to shorten the distance and lower the cost and time it took for ships to carry cargo between the Atlantic and Pacific Oceans. Before the canal, ships would have to go around the entire continent of South America, which added approximately 12,000 miles to each voyage.

The Panama Canal is known as a lock-type canal. It connects the Atlantic and Pacific Oceans via the narrow Isthmus of Panama.

The canal lock system makes it possible for Navy ships, as well as other cargo and cruise ships, to cross an otherwise impassable area, since there are no naturally occurring rivers, lakes, or oceans near the canal. Locks are in place over the 40-mile stretch of the canal. The locks would be filled with water, lowered, and lifted, and then the ship would be moved forward by the mechanism. It was fascinating to watch the process.

Crewmembers of the dock landing ship USS Pearl Harbor (LSD 52) are at their stations on the bow as the ship awaits entry into the Panama Canal's Mira Flores Locks in Panama City, Panama, on April 6, 2007. Pearl Harbor is transiting the Canal during the Partnership of the Americas 2007 exercise.

Twenty-seven days later, on February 14, 1991, we arrived at our home port of Pearl Harbor. It was a beautiful, sunny Hawaiian day, and the ship's entire crew manned the rails in our dress white uniforms as we sailed around the island of Oahu and entered Naval Station Pearl Harbor. From the docks, families lined up to cheer and wave, with a Navy band playing music in the background as the ship came closer. It was good to be back in Hawaii for the second time in my Navy career. My girlfriend and her daughter were on the pier with the other families to welcome our ship to our new home. It was a beautiful homecoming.

While our ship's hull number was actually CG-65, we were at sea so much in those early days we referred to the Chosin as CG-365, because we were at sea nearly every day of the year. Our captain really wanted to make admiral that year, so he kept the ship at sea in naval exercises to prepare and train us for our first full deployment.

In August 1991, we departed Pearl Harbor and deployed to the Western Pacific, Indian Ocean, and Persian Gulf for Operation Southern Watch with the USS Ranger CV-61 aircraft carrier battle group that included six ships and a submarine. Operation Southern Watch was an air-centric military operation for monitoring and controlling airspace to enforce Iraqi no-fly zones. The United Nations Security Council had demanded that Iraq put an end to a long period of repressing its citizens. The Council hoped that by putting pressure on the country, it would encourage—or force—positive movement on human and political rights issues. Pressure mounted when, following the end of the Gulf War, the Iraqi Air Force attacked Shi'ite Muslims in the southern part of the country. Essentially, we were trying to keep the Iraq military from invading its neighbors by offering air cover with our anti-air warship.

Our cryptologic and signals intelligence operations were 24/7, action-packed and directly contributed to the success of the mission. On board our ship, we had Arabic interpreters and other signals intelligence collectors working overtime to keep us up to speed. As a cryptologic technician, communications, it was my job to ensure that all secured communications and electronic equipment was up and operational, and that classified intercepts and messages were transmitted and delivered in a timely matter. With our specialized cryptologic kits, we had the capability to detect airborne threats before they reached our ship or battle group radar systems, which gave advanced protection and operational awareness to the USS Chosin and other ships within our battle group. I was immensely proud to be serving our military and country at this important time in our history.

The deployment to the Persian Gulf was a long one, from August 1991 through February 1992. During this time at sea, I missed celebrating all major holidays at home—including Veteran's Day, Halloween, Thanksgiving, Christmas, New Years, as well as my birthday. On major holidays while at sea, the ship's captain and chaplain lead and commemorate or celebrate with special meals, decorations, and other activities to boost morale. During the six months, we had ports of call in Hong Kong, Thailand, Australia, and the Marshall Islands. We even anchored out at the Republic of Kiribati, a 33-island chain in the Pacific, home to the city of Tarawa, which was breathtaking. The water and beaches are majestic and the view, even from the ship, looked like a scene from heaven.

During that six-month deployment, I was promoted from an E-6 rank to E-7 chief petty officer. Making chief is a major milestone in the Navy. At that point, the uniform changes. Rank is recognized by the insignia on your collar (i.e., the Navy anchors). Achieving one's anchors in the Navy is a significant accomplishment as chiefs run the Navy.

As the chief, I served as the Ships Signals Exploitation Space (SSES) communications division chief and the ship's education services officer (ESO). As the ESO, I had access to the enlisted sailors' test scores and other education-related documentation,

Chief Petty Officer photo onboard USS Chosin CG-65.

and I was astonished by the data and information in these files. Many of the sailors with lower test scores were minorities. I had a feeling they came from a similar background as me and may have had similar experiences as I had growing up on Cherry Street. After all, many enlisted personnel came from rural or inner-city areas. I knew firsthand that there were not many opportunities in those areas, given my own experience. I also knew how much of a difference a formal education and training could make in a person's life. I was inspired to do whatever I could to help the young sailors in prioritizing their personal growth and development through education.

I thought back to my interaction with the young lady I had met earlier in my career—the one I had thought was in college but who, in fact, was only in high school. That interaction helped me to understand and appreciate the importance of and difference an education could have on one's self-confidence and station in life.

So, I established the Professional Excellence Academy onboard the USS Chosin, a program, which became near and dear to my heart. It was designed to encourage and expand the professional growth and development of our junior sailors. In the program, we assisted young sailors and prepared them for advancement. A few of the chiefs just wanted their sailors to work hard and get the job done. I respected that, but I also knew that helping them in their professional development would have a lasting positive impact on both the individual and our overall mission.

I recall one young sailor who was 19 years old and from Brooklyn, New York, who I will refer to as S.R.B. S.R.B. was an undesignated deck seaman, meaning he did not have a specialized or trained skill (i.e., combat systems, operations specialist, or engineer). Deck seamen perform critical work on the ship, and they are generally in charge of mooring the ship to the pier or anchoring while at sea and steering the ship. Other duties include cleaning, painting, securing, and maintaining equipment safely and properly, which all are extremely important aspects to preserving a Navy ship. S.R.B. stuck out to me because he had the lowest basic skills test scores of the entire crew. I took a liking to S.R.B. because he was a good-natured, affable young man, and he was interested in self-development and improvement.

One day we were in port at Pearl Harbor, and I saw him at the forward part of the ship near the missile launchers, where he was painting. "S.R.B., how are you?" I asked.

"I am great, Chief, how are you?"

"I'm fine. First, thank you for participating in the basic skills testing. I reviewed your test scores and wanted to know if you would be interested in joining our Professional Excellence Academy Program?"

And without hesitation, he said, "I heard about the program and yes, of course, I would like to join."

I said, "Great, let me talk to Boats." Boats is short for the chief boatswain's mate, the chief in charge of all the deck seamen, and who is generally the most respected in the Chief's Mess. Talking with Boats, well, that was an entirely different exchange. Boats became angry when I informed him that S.R.B. would participate in the program because Boats had wanted him topside on the paint crew. Boats pushed back, but, in the end, S.R.B. did participate in the program, and he was among the most excited and appreciative for the opportunity to learn.

At this point in my career and evolution as an expert in cryptologic communications, I finally felt confident as a leader and Navy professional. I was now "the Chief," and it felt good.

On my first performance evaluation, I was ranked among the top chief petty officers on board the entire ship.

In writing, my captain praised me with words I still treasure to this day, saying, "Everything Chief Earl touches turns to gold."

When I read those words, my heart swelled with confidence in all my hard work. I had had some difficult challenges and many successes, and his words were powerful. The Navy captain, who was later promoted to admiral, meant what he said. At the time, I did not quite grasp the impact his opinion had on me, but 30 years later, I realize I continued to strive to live up to that opinion. It played a major role in shaping my confidence as a naval cryptologist.

I also earned my enlisted surface warfare specialist (ESWS) qualification onboard the USS Chosin. It was a voluntary program that required participants to learn about every aspect of a Navy ship, from weapon systems to propulsion, engineering, electronics, navigation, damage control, and everything in between. That was well outside my scope as a cryptologist, but it was critical to obtain the qualification given the fierce and competitive nature of the Navy's promotion system at the senior enlisted levels. Given that the USS Chosin is a guided missile cruiser, a highly capable and complex warship, it was an intense experience—but it was one that served to build my confidence in my leadership abilities and my understanding of Navy ships.

We supported many cryptologic and intelligence operations at the tactical, strategic, and national level. Though much of our work remains classified to this day, I can tell you that we provided special intelligence communications, signals intelligence, and operational intelligence to the ship's leadership, combat information center, the National Security Agency and other higher echelon entities, including the White House.

We spent so much time at sea that I did not have much time to enjoy Hawaii the way I had in the early 1980s. But I had evolved in many ways and dedicated myself to self-improvement and committed to the Navy's mission, and its core values of honor, courage, and commitment, and professional excellence. I had finally seen how hard work, solid character, integrity, self-reliance, and perseverance worked together to build confidence.

CHAPTER 9

INTROSPECTION

Naval Security Station - 3801 Nebraska Avenue,
Washington D.C.

Definition: *Introspection is an examination of one's own thoughts and feelings.*[18]

I returned to the Naval Security Station, 3801 Nebraska Avenue, Washington D.C. in 1994. This would be my second tour of duty in D.C., but I now held a more senior position. I arrived as a chief petty officer (E-7), but I soon received official notification that I was promoted to senior chief petty officer (E-8). In a little less than three years, I had advanced from E-6 to E-8. I was promoted extraordinarily fast during times when promotions were highly competitive and difficult to achieve.

---

18 Introspection is an examination of one's own thoughts and feelings   https://www.merriam-webster.com/dictionary/introspection

Following the announcement of the promotion results, a large town hall meeting was hosted by the selection board panel members to share their feedback and perspectives with all the chief petty officers. I was one of only two promotions of the nearly fifty or so eligible personnel for E-8 and E-9 that were assigned to the headquarters compound. Only two promotions were surprisingly low because many of the top senior enlisted cryptologists were assigned to the headquarters, and generally most were the best in our highly competitive cryptology fields. And I was clearly among the absolute best Navy-wide.

Formerly the Naval Security Station located at 3801 Nebraska Avenue Washington D.C., now the Headquarters for the U.S. Department of Homeland Security (DHS).

As I walked back alone from the office building following the meeting, four other chiefs confronted me. One of them approached me with a hint of sarcasm and a tone that spoke of indifference and jealousy.

"What makes you so special?" he asked, surrounded by his buddies.

His friends smirked, waiting for an answer. Inside, I bristled. He did not have to spell it out that he was implying my race had played a factor. Back then, I was one of the few African Americans in a senior leadership position within the cryptologic community. I knew he was trying to provoke me, and it was tempting to react, but I remained calm and collected as I had learned my lesson about taking matters into my own hands, so to speak. Instead, I looked him squarely in the face.

"You know, it's not that I'm so special," I said. "It's just that you a-holes are just *that* bad."

I then paused and looked around at each of them, taking in the stunned look on their faces before walking off. Although I knew that I could not singlehandedly fix the huge problem of prejudice and bigotry, I had decided long ago that I would do what I could to deal with it on the spot when it reared its head. I think the marine gunnery sergeant who had looked out for me in Pensacola, Florida would have been pleased. I had come a long way from that young sailor running away from the military police and hiding on top of a building.

A promotion ceremony was held for me and the other selectee some time afterwards which my family, girlfriend, and colleagues enthusiastically attended. This was a significant career milestone, especially given my humble beginnings and challenging start in the Navy.

I was now living in Alexandria, Virginia, which was 11 miles from the Naval Security Station, only about a 25-minute drive, which was a great commute for the Washington D.C. Metro Area. The

D.C. homicide rate had remained high at around 400 murders per year, but this was at least substantially down from the peak of 482 murders in 1991. Life and work for me was great. In my free time, my girlfriend, her daughter, and I would visit my favorite places like Old Town Alexandria, historical parks, landmarks, and the many restaurants in the D.C. Metro Area. We would often travel to South Carolina to visit my mother and sister.

Assigned to a senior leadership position, I oversaw our special intelligence communications operations that included about 25 personnel, and I also served as a technical advisor. My organization and the Naval Security Group headquarters staff were in the planning and coordination phases for the physical move and relocation of our cryptologic headquarters to Fort George G. Meade, Maryland.

Along with my assigned duties and responsibilities, I also established the Naval Security Station's Professional Excellence Academy, a program almost identical to the one I founded while onboard the USS Chosin, back in Hawaii, however, there were more classes and the participation level was slightly larger. The program was tremendously successful, so much so that the top enlisted representative, the force master chief, invited me to outline and brief the program to all the commanding officers and command master chiefs of the cryptologic community during their annual conference.

Later I was asked to roll out the Professional Excellence Academy for the entire cryptologic community, which included approximately two thousand personnel stationed in many naval security group departments and detachments throughout the world. I was honored to then have the opportunity to have a direct and positive impact on an entire community of sailors in their professional growth, development, and advancement.

Just months into the implementation of the program, I received official word that I was selected for the Navy Enlisted Education Advancement Program. The program was a two-year opportunity for highly qualified and career-motivated enlisted personnel to earn an associate's or bachelor's degree depending on their educational status. At the time of my selection, I had only a few college credit hours. Though I have led, mentored, guided, and promoted many sailors throughout my career, I had not earned a college degree.

Educational challenges like mine can still be found in the military today. In 2018, the *Military Times* found that overall, the number of troops using tuition assistance from all five services had fallen.[19] Since the Defense Department started tracking its usage across service branches in 2015, the number of troops using tuition assistance has fallen 14.5 percent. Why? Part of the answer can be found in budget constraints. The Navy, for example, stopped accepting new tuition assistance enrollments in the 2019 fiscal year after spending around $77 million to fund the benefit, which was approximately $2 million dollars more than was budgeted, according to the *Military Times*.

Some experts also theorize that the falling number of the enrolled can be attributed to a shrinking military. Still others suggest that it might have something to do with the strong economy the U.S. enjoyed before the COVID-19 pandemic, as college enrollment tends to increase when the economy tanks and decreases when the

19 Fewer troops are using Tuition Assistance benefits (militarytimes.com).

economy is doing well. My opinion is that education is critical to our personal and professional development and should be prioritized if at all possible. Yes, continuing an education is a personal decision. For me, I recognized when I left South Carolina and arrived in California, that I needed to put my education first and I was determined to do so. This was a challenge back then, however, because many military leaders did not always encourage or set an example for young service members. And of course, it is difficult to do so in combat zones and during military deployments but developing an educated military force should be a priority and a core value with regard to sustaining our national security and doing the best for our troops.

Since that time, I have recognized exactly how deep the education gap was between South Carolina and California, and the rest of the U.S., for that matter. Education had been extremely important to me. I had been serving overseas, stationed on two Navy ships, and working to improve the education and experience of those who were in my charge. Now I had a chance to earn a degree.

But it was not that cut and dry. I was now facing a major personal and professional dilemma. Was I going to accept my selection and attend college for two years, or was I going to stay to set up the academy to continue helping other sailors advance in their own education and careers? It was an incredibly stressful period and time of deep introspection about my next step and path forward. I had to make an important decision. I weighed both the pros and cons, and after some deep reflection, I found that my education was too important to me to decline and pass on the opportunity for self-improvement and personal development at this pivotal point in my life and career. I had sacrificed so much at that point.

So, I made up my mind that I would accept the offer. I then scheduled a meeting with the force master chief.

On the day of the meeting, I was terribly anxious. I did not know how the force master chief would react. As I entered his office, I noticed his demeanor was friendly and a bit jovial, which was not his normal disposition. His office was beautiful, with leather chairs and walls filled with pictures, awards, and other memorabilia. He asked me to have a seat.

"So, what's on your mind?" He asked. He did not know specifically why I was there.

I was uneasy, but I decided not to beat around the bush. "Well, Master Chief, I have been selected for the two-year Navy Enlisted Education Advancement Program, and I have decided to accept. It will start in about three months' time," I said.

He looked at me, an expression of shock creeping across his face. "What about the academy implementation?"

I told him I could work with him to find a replacement. But before I could finish responding fully, he turned red and interrupted me. "You can't accept this two-year program. The Navy and these sailors need you!"

I expressed my appreciation for this endorsement and the support for the academy and the sailors but explained that this was something I had to do for myself. I had spent nearly 13 years dedicated to the Navy's mission and leading and developing other sailors. Now it was time for me to prioritize my own growth and educational development. I had worked long and exceptionally hard, and now I wanted to take advantage of this opportunity that

I had earned. I went further and stated that he has had a long and storied career and had earned a master's degree, I believe it was an MBA. I wanted to do the same. He was not pleased.

"You do this, and you won't ever make master chief," he said.

That stung, but I knew I was making the right choice for myself. I looked him in the eyes, and said, "Roger that, Master Chief, but my education and professional development at this time are much more important to me than being promoted. I am grateful to be a senior chief. I have given my all to these sailors, but it is time for me to go to college full time, and when I return, I will be an even better example for them to follow."

He looked at me, gave me a hard stare, and wished me luck as I walked out of the door.

Later, I transitioned my duties and responsibilities and provided the implementation framework for the Professional Excellence Academy to a fellow chief petty officer. I then registered and was accepted to Northern Virginia Community College's two-year degree program at the Alexandria Campus, which was only one mile from my residence on Merton Court.

During the two-year program, I attended classes full time to obtain the 60 hours required. I took the education process seriously and during that time had the opportunity to assist academic counselors and even some of the professors in providing students with personal and professional advice. I also was selected for *Who's Who in America's Junior Colleges 1998*, and elected vice president of Phi Theta Kappa, International Honor Society, Tau Nu Chapter. I eventually graduated magna cum laude with an associate of science degree.

I was a little older than some of the other students, but I did not stick out. I had already developed life and leadership skills that gave me a leg up in navigating the world of academics. I particularly enjoyed the elective philosophy courses in which we studied Aristotle, Niccolò Machiavelli, Socrates, and other philosophers.

As part of the Navy's Enlisted Education Advancement Program, on the first Saturday of each month, I had to don my Navy uniform and perform general military duties at Anacostia Naval Station near Downtown Washington D.C. I was the senior Navy leader among the other student naval personnel, and I generally directed the group. Typically, we would conduct military training exercises, discuss Navy policy guidance reviews and changes, and group academic support sessions. Because the participants were enrolled in as many as 10 different colleges and universities in the Washington D.C. Metropolitan region, we fed off one another's energy levels and learned from each other's experiences.

After completing the associate degree, I could say with certainty that I was glad I had made the decision to accept the two-year program and had resisted the pressure exerted by the force master chief. Through introspection and tenacity regarding my goals of self-development and improvement, I was able to make the right choice. It was not so much obtaining the associate's degree, but rather the discipline and attention to detail in the formal education process that gave me the tools to learn how to study, conduct research and generally learn how to be a student—all the things I never challenged myself to do in high school. Immediately upon graduation from Northern Virginia Community College, I received official orders to Naval Security Group Department, Dededo, Guam, USA.

Though all was going well professionally, my girlfriend and I had officially ended our nine-year relationship. She had remained in the Navy at the cryptologic headquarters where we had met in 1987, while I was headed to Guam. Upon reflection, though we had discussed marriage, the challenges of us both serving in the military, the travel, the responsibilities, work stresses, separations, and just life in general all contributed to the difficulties we had in sustaining our relationship. She has since retired from the U.S. Navy and now lives in Maryland.

CHAPTER 10

DETERMINATION

Naval Security Group Department, Guam USA

*"You may not control all the events that happen to you, but you can
decide not to be reduced by them."*

—Maya Angelou

I n August 1996, I arrived on Guam, an unincorporated U.S. terri-
tory located in the Western Pacific Ocean. Guam is the largest of
the Mariana Islands with a population of fewer than 170,000 people.
It was an 8,000-mile flight from Columbia, S.C. with two layovers,
one in California and one in Hawaii. I lost almost two days due to
the long flight and 15-hour time difference from the East Coast. A
beautiful island with jungles, mountains, and beaches, Guam is only
36 miles long and 12 miles wide and has an established Chamorro
culture and heritage. It is also a top tourist destination and wedding
location for visitors from Japan and other Asian countries, as well
as Europe.

I reported to the Naval Security Group Department in Dededo, located at the U.S. Naval Computer and Telecommunications Station on the northern end of the island near Andersen Air Force Base. The military installation was huge but mainly consisted of undeveloped land and very few facilities. There seemed to be more communications transmitters and satellite antennas than buildings and people.

Naval Communications and Telecommunications Station, Dededo, Guam. Satellite Communctaions site.

As a senior chief, I was the leading chief petty officer in charge of a 70-member organization that provided special intelligence communications and messaging support services for extremely sensitive real-time cryptologic and signals intelligence operations.[20]

We worked in a windowless building located inside a very large Wullenweber circular antenna array system used for radio direction finding, designed to triangulate radio signals for navigation,

---

20 Signals Intelligence (SIGINT) is intelligence derived from electronic signals and systems used by foreign targets, such as communications systems, radars, and weapons systems. SIGINT provides a vital window for our nation into foreign adversaries' capabilities, actions, and intentions.

cryptologic collection, intelligence gathering, and search and rescue. Because of the large antenna arrays that looked like a circular
fence, we commonly referred to the Wullenweber system as the
elephant cage. I recall when I initially arrived and saw it for the
first time, it was eerie—it felt like a different planet or something
out of a space movie. The antenna array towers were over 400 feet
high, and their number seemed endless, maybe 70 or 80, and that
is only counting the large antennas. There was only one entry and
one exit, and both were highly secured. To reach the entry you had
to go down a long two-lane road and even today I still get goose-
bumps when I picture the scenery of that drive and the tactical
and national security operations we performed during that time.

At the elephant cage, we conducted foreign intelligence signals
collection, gathering information from radio communications,
cell towers, satellites, and more. We were responsible for passing
critical information to the NSA, and sometimes even to the
White House.

*Naval Security Group Department Guam. Wullenweber Circular Antenna
Array System aka Elephant Cage.*

The Navy has a saying that goes "hit the deck running." That is exactly what I did when I reported as the leading chief petty officer. In my first 90 days, I conducted an evaluation of the operations, morale, and overall culture. I interviewed every sailor within the Communications Division. After meeting with the department head, and based on my own immediate observations, it was clear that drastic changes were needed. I met with the two division chiefs both individually and as a group.

I greeted them. "Good morning, Chiefs. As you are aware, I am conducting my initial evaluation and assessment of our organization and would appreciate your candor and transparency."

"Understood, Senior Chief," they both replied.

"Okay, so, generally speaking, how are operations and the overall morale of the division?"

Again, they both spoke up with a consistent refrain and position. "Senior Chief, operations are great, and morale is high overall."

"Can you all think of any adjustments that we could or should make to increase our professional excellence as a division?"

Their collective response was, "None that we can think of."

The chiefs' positions on these matters contrasted quite a bit with the large majority of the subordinate and junior personnel. And, quite frankly, I had anticipated that that would be the case.

Central to the problem was that the senior leadership were on a first name basis with junior personnel and favoritism was apparent within the ranks, which contributed to what I assessed to be mediocre operational performance, low professional standards, and low morale. On the positive side, the team demonstrated strong technical expertise and talent.

The Navy had, and still has, strict fraternization rules for good reason, and many of those rules were being disregarded. In many cases, some of those in senior leaders took advantage of their positions in an effort to bolster their own power and image. The chief of naval operations defines fraternization as a gender-neutral concept used to identify personal relationships that do not respect the bounds of acceptable senior-subordinate relationships.[21] Personal relationships between officers and enlisted members that are unduly familiar and that do not respect differences in grade or rank are prohibited. This rule largely extends to include senior enlisted chief petty officers and subordinate personnel as well. Unfortunately, there are many cases where military organizations fail in this regard, and confidence is lost. Favoritism, lack of professionalism and bad morale are corrosive to good order and the discipline necessary for high standards within the military ranks. This was a serious matter, especially given the importance of the national security operations of the group to which we were assigned, I knew things needed to change, and fast.

For many young sailors, it was their first time away from home. In addition, some of them had married young and just did not know a lot about life in general. Without positive, disciplined leadership helping to guide their path, they faced many challenges in balancing life, their military commitments, and even just living on a small island thousands of miles away from home.

---

21 The Navy's policies on fraternization are contained in OPNAV Instruction 5370.2B, Navy Fraternization Policy.

On one occasion, for example, I received a phone call in the middle of the night. One of the sailors assigned to our division had been detained by military police and she could only be released under my authority as the leading chief. When I arrived, I learned that the sailor had been detained for a verbal assault on her husband, who was also a sailor within the department, but not in our communications intelligence division. They lived in Navy base housing, and apparently that night they had had an argument and she had forced him out of the home. That does not sound overly unusual as disagreements are generally typical in young marriages, except for the fact he was not fully clothed, so basically naked, and afraid. Understandably embarrassed and ashamed, he went to a neighbor's home nearby for safety. Apparently, there had been ongoing physical and verbal abuse for quite some time, but he did not tell anyone until the events of that night. Both sailors received formal administrative actions, professional and marriage counseling assistance from the Navy's Family Services Center, which I organized. And this is just one example of the type of incident that occurred in the early days of my assignment.

I instituted improvements in processes and procedures within the division and our operations to establish order and direction to the team. Truth be told, I was not having an easy time of it myself. Life on a small island in the middle of the Western Pacific Ocean was challenging for everyone. In those days, I thought a lot about home, particularly of my mother. Four years earlier, while getting dressed for Sunday service my mother had had a massive stroke and was later found lying on the floor by a close friend and neighbor. Though she survived the stroke, she was paralyzed on her right side. My sister and my niece moved from Washington, D.C. back to South Carolina to help care for her. I often worried

Determination

that I would get the dreaded phone call that something terrible happened to her.

One morning, while at work, I received a phone call in my office. I was being summoned to the executive officer office at the headquarters facility near the main gate—about a four-mile drive from the elephant cage. I was not told any specifics about the summons, just that it was an emergency and I needed to get there as soon as possible. As I drove alone to the headquarters building, I was already in tears. It *had* to be bad news about my mother. I felt a deep dread building in the pit of my stomach.

When I arrived, the executive assistant escorted me into the suite. Not only was the executive officer there, standing in front of his desk, but so was the command master chief and the command managed equal opportunity officer. The pit in my stomach grew as tears welled in my eyes. The executive officer asked me to sit down, and I complied. Then the conversation took a turn I did not expect.

The executive officer, in a stern, directive tone, told me they had received an anonymous report about me from the U.S. Navy hotline back in D.C. He began to read the summary of the report aloud. In the report, it was stated that I was contentious and intimidating, and that personnel were afraid and uncomfortable with the changes being made in the division. After reading the summary, the executive officer raised his head to look at me.

"I see you are messing things up within the Special Intelligence Communications Division," he said. "What do you have to say for yourself?"

I was in total shock. I stood up. "You're goddam right, sir. Yes, I am messing things up for everybody," I said. "I came down here thinking you had news about my mother, and you're talking about an anonymous hotline phone call? Let me tell you, things are not right here. Yes, you have that right, I'm messing things up for everybody."

 I let them all have it. I could not believe they were making a big deal about an anonymous phone call. But it was the way they came at me that was the last straw.

Their stance was accusatory, severe, and unsupportive. They were poised to take some sort of administrative action against me because some person had left a baseless and unsubstantiated anonymous complaint that I was intimidating the sailors, among other things.

"So, you are saying that you are in fact messing things up?" The Executive Officer asked me. He seemed astonished.

"That's exactly right, sir," I said. "And this hotline call needs to be investigated. I can provide you a 90-day assessment that documents all my findings and recommendations for change given all the unprofessional shenanigans that have being ongoing in that division."

A couple weeks later, the person who made the anonymous hotline call came forward on their own accord. I am not sure if it was out of guilt or a sudden change of conscience, but she told the official conducting the inquiry that her superiors had directed her to report me to the Navy hotline.

The inquiry further uncovered that it was a plan and conspiracy to undermine, discredit, and potentially remove me from my position as the division leading chief petty officer because those who were in charge before my arrival were intimidated by my presence and wanted their power and influence back.

Given the serious nature of the matter, the inquiry official provided me with the option of removing or placing aside some of the leadership and personnel involved in the scheme. Strategically, I decided to keep them all right where they were so I could deal with the matter internally. I did make several key personnel changes and organizational structure shifts. I then refocused on our mission objectives, which were centered around professional growth and development among all members of the division, for the purpose of achieving collective excellence. There were some growing pains, but eventually the chiefs and the other members aligned appropriately under my vision and direction. We later turned the division around and established professional excellence. As a result, promotions skyrocketed, and morale, teamwork, and performance were at an all-time high.

But my challenges did not end there. The command master chief was not too fond of me. It was clear he did not like my disposition, and I suspected he did not like how I had stood up to him and the executive officer. And the posturing between the two of us continued throughout my two-year tour of duty. I found him to be somewhat of a tyrant. He had to control everything and everyone, and we did not like each other. But he also could not deny the high levels of performance that had been achieved by the cryptologic team supporting the mission.

I was among the most competent chief petty officers and leaders within the Naval Security Group department. Nonetheless, I managed to resist conforming to the command master chief's bullying, bias, and borderline resentful nature. I refused to let him walk all over me, like he did with others. I was determined to stand up for myself.

Many of the other chiefs did not want to cross the master chief—he was essentially was responsible for and influenced the positioning of our ranking, which was a key element in the promotion of chiefs to senior chief and master chief level. Some of the other chiefs were so fearful of the master chief that they would avoid me if they knew he was around since they knew we did not see eye to eye. One afternoon, I was playing pool with a fellow chief when the master chief walked in. Suddenly, my fellow chief dropped his pool stick on the table and left.

"I can't be seen hanging out with you," he said. I looked at him. I could not believe how little courage the man had.

"Hey, I understand," I said. "You have to do what you have to do." I finished the game alone and left.

I worked long hours as a normal course of business. I also spent time each day studying to get the credits I needed to inch my way closer to a bachelor's degree. Even though I was busy, I had to stay at the top of my game—always. It is not like I was walking on eggshells, but I knew if I made a mistake or found myself in another conflict with the master chief, things could become considerably more difficult for me.

Despite the rigors of my time on the base, overall, life was good for me. I lived in a spacious, three-bedroom condo in the village of Tamuning, near the beach and the economic center of Guam where the large hotels lay, attracting the tourists. The weather was great, and I enjoyed weekend trips around the island in my white 1996 Volkswagen Passat, with the sunroof down.

To stay in shape, I was active in sports, specifically basketball and softball. I was one of the top basketball players on the base, but softball was more popular in Guam, hands down. I organized and managed an annual softball tournament, raising several thousand dollars in sponsorship and support from local business owners and charities backed by the chiefs. It was a "big deal" and extraordinarily successful.

Although my work activities had normalized, I still found myself regularly on my guard given the climate within the chiefs' mess. Nevertheless, two major events changed everything in that year.

First, in August 1997, Korean Air Flight 801[22] crashed on Nimitz Hill on its approach to the airport in Asan, Guam, killing 229 of the 254 passengers aboard. This was headline news for quite a while. The National Transportation Safety Board believed that poor communication between the flight crew was probable cause for the crash, along with the pilot's poor decision making on the approach landing. The Korean community was both outraged and hurt by this tragic accident.

Then, in December of that same year, Guam was struck by Super Typhoon Paka.[23] This was Mother Nature at her worst. It hit the island at night with average sustained winds of 175 mph. One

---

22 https://www.ntsb.gov/investigations/AccidentReports/Reports/AAR0001.pdf.
23 Super typhoon Paka smashes military quarters Naval Station Marianas, Guam. (defense.gov).

wind gust recorded at nearby Andersen Air Force Base was the strongest ever recorded on earth at 236 mph, and the heavy winds and rainfall lasted for days.

Military quarters in the Nimitz Hill housing area near Naval Station Marianas, Guam, lie smashed in the aftermath of super typhoon Paka on Dec. 17, 1997.

I hunkered down in my condo which was a hurricane-proof structure, but I was scared. The noise was deafening, and it was terrible not knowing what was going on outside. I was stuck inside for several days. All night long, I heard the howling winds hit the island, leaving destruction in their wake. Roofs caved in and debris crashed all around. It sounded as though the world were coming to an end. When the storm ended, walking outside was dangerous—debris, power lines and pools were everywhere.

For weeks after the storm, there was no power, no electricity, limited telephone service, and no water pressure. Homes and businesses had to use portable generators borrowed from government and military facilities.

All in all, there were millions of dollars in damages that destroyed about 1,500 buildings and damaged 10,000 more; 5,000 people were left homeless, and the island experienced a complete power outage. Guam government officials announced that Super Typhoon Paka had wreaked damaged worth an estimated $385 million.

Though our work facilities used emergency generators to maintain critical operations, much of our mission and operations were severely impacted. Some of our special operations never fully recovered, and most were shifted to alternate sites and/or were being managed at a remote location.

Because of the devastation it caused, Super Typhoon Paka had changed many perspectives in terms of understanding what really mattered in life. Community service, teamwork and supporting one another seemed to be the priority for all in the storm's aftermath. I lead the organization to ensure the good health and general welfare of the sailors.

My assignment in Guam was tough, but I was determined to be successful. I was determined to do the absolute best for the Navy's mission, and I accomplished that. Everyone was better for it, even if I stepped on a few toes and lost a few friends along the way. If there is one thing I know how to do, it is to build successful programs.

I was slated to return to the U.S. for my next assignment and rotation, but instead I received orders to report to the staff of the Commander, Submarine Group Seven, in Yokosuka, Japan. I did not have the opportunity to fly back home to South Carolina to visit with my mother. I went directly from Guam to Yokosuka.

That is why they refer to them as orders, I did not have a choice in the matter. At least not this time.

CHAPTER 11

THE CONCEPT OF BEING ME

Commander Submarine Group Seven,
Yokosuka, Japan

"Be who you are and say what you feel, because those who mind don't
matter, and those who matter don't mind."
—**Bernard M. Baruch**

In August 1998, after a three-hour flight from Guam, I landed at the Narita International Airport in Tokyo, Japan. This was my third time flying into Narita, so I felt less bewildered by my surroundings than I had after my initial arrival 13 years earlier. My new assignment would mark my second tour of duty in Japan and was yet another opportunity to support the submarine community, commonly referred to as the silent service.

The Commander, Submarine Group Seven's[24] mission is to direct submarine operations and activities throughout the Western Pacific, Indian Ocean, and Arabian Sea. The group included two forward-deployed submarine tenders, the USS Frank Cable (AS-40) and USS Emory S. Land (AS-39), five surveillance towed array sensor system vessels, three oceanographic survey vessels tasked for theater anti-submarine warfare operations, and four attack submarines which were homeported in Guam.

Philiippine Sea (June 14, 2020). The Los Angeles-class fast-attack submarine USS Asheville (SSN-758) transits alongside the U.S. 7th Fleet flagship USS Blue Ridge (LCC-19) during a submarine familiarization (SUBFAM) training. U.S. Navy photo by Mass Communication Specialist Seaman Brandon L. Harris/Released.

I served as the communications department's leading chief petty officer and was soon thereafter promoted to master chief. Yes, master chief petty officer (E-9). That was a big deal. I had achieved the highest enlisted rank in the military where I was now among the top 1.25 percent of the enlisted members in the Navy and

24 Commander Submarine Group 7. https://www.csp.navy.mil/csg7/About-COMSUBGRU-SEVEN/.

leaders within the cryptologic community. This was, by far, one of the most significant professional achievements in my lifetime.

Cryptologic technician (communications) master chief petty officer portrait.

I had come full circle. Having started out as a mere E-2 submarine broadcast operator only a few short years ago, I was now in Japan serving the country, leading, and supporting classified operations at a high level. Yes, I was proud to be the master chief, but more so grateful, when I reflected on my humble beginnings back on Cherry Street.

Commanded by a rear admiral, our staff was small, but our work was important and extremely sensitive as it supported both tactical operations and strategic national security programs. I served as the special intelligence communications division officer.

Our then chief of staff was a very sharp, squared-away professional. He was a former enlisted member—just like me—who had converted to the officer ranks. He constantly tried to encourage me to convert to officer, like he had done earlier in his career. Although it was flattering to know he thought so highly of me, he simply did not understand why I did not want to take the officer path as I enjoyed being the master chief and the respect earned for being the top enlisted, but he was persistent. Each time he approached me about the subject, I politely declined his offer. It had reached a point where I would purposefully avoid running into him to prevent having that conversation *again.*

The deadline for submissions for the chief warrant officer packages was nearing, and on this particular day, he caught me in the hallway, and. I must state, I was not having a good day.

The truth is, I genuinely enjoyed my rank as master chief. I had worked so hard to get there, surmounting incredible odds, and I did not want to change course.

"Master chief, the packages are due on Friday, and I need your package on my desk by close of business tomorrow," he said. I snapped. Frustrated by his persistence, coupled with the difficult day I was having, all pretenses melted away.

"How many times do I have to tell you, sir? I am a master chief, and chiefs run the Navy," I said. "I have no desire to be an officer and a gentleman." As the heat of annoyance rose in his cheeks, his face turned red. He may have been caught off guard by the sharpness in my reply, but my answer should not have been a surprise.

"Fine, master chief!" he said as he turned away from me. And that was finally the end of that. It took a while for him to understand, but he eventually understood my lack of interest and realized that being a master chief meant a lot to me both personally and professionally. Besides, master chiefs can be much grumpier, and I liked that much better because as part of the role we were generally expected to speak our minds without consequences and repercussions. There is no such thing as an E-10, and master chief was the highest enlisted rank one could obtain.

I lived off-base in a vibrant community near the Kita-Kurihama train station in Yokosuka. There were very few Americans living in my neighborhood, it was mostly Japanese families with children.

Engakuji Zen temple". One of Five Great Zen Temples (Gozan), close to Kita-Kamakura station. Taken in Kamakura, Japan - February 2018.

I appreciated so many things about the Japanese culture: the customs, food, traditions, and just the general courtesies extended towards one another. Although this may no longer be the case, I found that the Japanese were intrigued by Americans, particularly its younger generation. In my neighborhood it seemed I had celebrity-like status. As a case in point, *Esquire* magazine (Japan) featured me in their May 2000 issue with a full interview of me explaining my life in Japan. It included a picture of me sitting in my living room with my TV on. Interestingly, they seemed particularly fascinated with the details of things, and wanted to include things such as my blender, and they made sure to capture a picture of it in my kitchen. Note that in the U.S., the May 2000 version of *Esquire* featured former late-night TV host, David Letterman; in Japan it featured a master chief in the U.S. Navy.

I enjoyed my drives home after a long day at our secured facility. There was something so refreshing about leaving a day of high-intensity operations behind and seeing so many people who were friendly and respectful toward one another. It was so different from my experiences growing up and even in the Navy. In the Navy, subordinates *had* to respect those in more senior rank. There was an underlying compliance which was necessary to ensure order. But that felt so different from my neighbors living out their lives with deep respect for one another. Living in that environment felt almost meditative. It made my heart smile. It made me reflect on my own life and how I wanted to live—I knew I wanted to carry some of that experience with me when I left.

During evenings and weekends, I studied hard to complete my college course work. I finally earned a bachelor of science degree in information systems management from the University of Maryland, University College, Asian Division. My goal had been to complete my bachelor's degree before I retired from the Navy, and now I had finally achieved it.

I was proud of myself—it had taken a lot of time, dedication, and sacrifice, but I had done it. It would have been easy to listen to the narrative that I had to go to college right out of high school but that had not been a possibility for me. In fact, in my neighborhood, particularly on Cherry Street, it was rare for anyone to even consider college—the consistent refrain was, "Learn a trade."

Even though I had been in the Navy for quite some time, I was still acutely aware of society's expectations that you were supposed to go to college, get married, buy a house, and have children. That was the American Dream so many of us were sold then, and that is still the case today. And right up until this day, I have yet to conform to those societal expectations. In fact, Earl Nightingale has a quote, *"The opposite of courage in our society is not cowardice... it is conformity."* And he also is quoted as saying, *"Success is really nothing more than the progressive realization of a worthy ideal. This means that any person who knows what they are doing and where they are going is a success. Any person with a goal towards which they are working is a successful person."*[25]

If going to college straight out of high school, getting married, buying a house, and having children is the benchmark for success, then by those standards I would be considered a failure. However, I was able to make my own way, carve out my own path, and accomplish the goals I had set for myself, and I continue to thrive and work towards my greatest potential.

Until I arrived, the Special Intelligence Communications Division had gone without a senior leader with a cryptologic background for an extended period; the division and operations were basically being managed by a leading petty officer (E-6). When I took over, I noticed that both leadership and professional standards were low, a matter I could easily handle. The team, however, did have excep-

25 Earl Nightingale, The Strangest Secret, 1957.

tionally good levels of camaraderie and high morale—a refreshing change of pace from some of my previous duty stations.

But of course, being in the military stationed overseas was still difficult, for some, more than others. The leading petty officer (E-6) of the division was well-liked by the junior personnel, and he was doing an outstanding job. Unfortunately, he was having significant personal and marital problems.

He was an African American and his wife was Japanese. They had five young children. She was a stay-at-home mother while he worked hard serving our country and doing his level best. Living in Japan is quite expensive, particularly for enlisted personnel on a military salary, and having to support five children was obviously extremely challenging for him. After a while, he just was not himself, and I began to notice changes in his behavior. Then I received a phone call.

I was just leaving the base when a command duty officer called me and said my leading petty officer had had an argument with his wife, and I needed to get there as quickly as I could. So, I made a U-turn and headed to their residence in base housing. When I arrived, several Naval officials were there. I started speaking with his wife, trying to calm the situation and better understand how I may be able to assist. She told me that he had driven off, taking one of their younger sons with him. Not having indicated where he was going, she was understandably concerned because he had not only been angry but had also seemed disoriented.

While speaking with his wife, I received another call. Someone had found his car near the Seaside Club next to the Navy Lodge. I ran to my car and drove there as quickly as I could. Arriving on the scene, I noticed his car with the driver's-side door wide open, lights on, and the engine still running. A female officer and other security personnel were already there too.

"I think I hear crying," said the female officer.

We all ran towards the sea wall. Two of the security personnel climbed the sea wall, which was dark and in an unlit area. One of the security personnel yelled, "I see him." He had spotted the child standing on the rocks. Thankfully, the tide was low, or he could have been easily carried off into the cold, unforgiving ocean.

Additional military police and emergency response teams arrived on the scene and quickly scaled the wall to assist, but they did not find the leading petty officer. As best we could fathom, he must have scaled the wall with the child. It is still unclear what his intentions were with respect to his son, but the child was soaking wet and ice cold when the officers brought him back over the wall.

The Coast Guard and other Navy search and rescue units scoured the cold, dark water searching for the leading petty officer. They searched for three hours before they found his body. Given the events of the evening, his death was ruled a suicide by drowning.

The next morning, I was summoned to the Naval hospital to officially identify his body. They told me I did not have to look for long—just long enough to ensure an official identification, so that is what I did. They had him wrapped up in a white sheet from the chest down and I could only see his head, face, and shoulders. Except for a large abrasion on his forehead, he looked peaceful, like he could have been asleep.

It was painful for me. Although I had gained a lot of experience as a Navy leader, this was new ground. I not only had to demonstrate leadership for my sailors, but also provide compassion and support for his bereaved family. He left behind a wife and five beautiful children. I knew he had been in a lot of pain, and it saddened me that it ended this way. I felt a deep sense of sorrow as I looked at him. I questioned whether or not I could have done something differently. But what else could I have done? He had been assigned duties outside of our sensitive compartment information facility classified area due to security clearance reasons, but I would meet with him regularly to discuss how he was doing. We would check in, laugh, joke, and reflect on ways to best handle the challenges he was facing. We even took a few long walks around the base near our building.

Unfortunately, suicide is not uncommon in the military. According to a Department of Defense Suicide Event Report Annual Report, the age-standardized suicide rate was 20.2 per 100,000 in 2015 and is the second leading cause of death among active-duty service members.[26] But this was the first time I had experienced a suicide so close to home.

The report also outlined a number of psychosocial factors that are associated with suicide risk in the military. The most common individual stressors identified were relationship problems, administrative/legal issues, and workplace difficulties. Other medical conditions that are associated with an increased risk for suicide include traumatic brain injury (TBI), chronic pain, and sleep dis-

---

26 Department of Defense Suicide Event (SER)
    https://www.pdhealth.mil/sites/default/files/images/docs/DoDSER_2015_Annual_
    Report.pdf.

orders. These conditions can contribute substantially to increased suicide risk in affected individuals.[27]

Years later, I would face my own battles with grief and depression when my mother passed away. For months, I suffered in silence and did not share my pain with anyone. But reflecting on this experience I had had with the leading petty officer; I think I realized I needed help sooner than I would have otherwise. Seeing everything I had seen, I ultimately became a strong proponent of getting help when you need it. But back then, I did not yet fully understand the level of grief we as human beings can endure before real help is needed.

I presided over the leading petty officer's memorial service and spoke during the ceremony, lending support to his wife and family. They were devastated, as was our division. It was hard to take on that role, but I knew it was my duty. He was my sailor and I had to be there to lead, even in death.

Soon though, I was dealt another blow. Navy Family Services Center grief counselors informed me that some of the sailors were speculating that the leading petty officer took his own life because of the stress I had placed him under. After all, he had been telling them that he was working long, grueling hours at my request. And, of course, they were unaware of his personal and marital problems. Part of me understood their making me the target— they were looking for answers and reasons for this painful tragedy. But it was not true, and I knew I had to stop the spread of rumors and misinformation. The next day, I held a mandatory all-hands meeting with the staff. I told them I had heard the rumors float-

27 Suicide in the Military. Center for Deployment Psychology.

ing around about our beloved shipmate, friend, and colleague. I explained that he had been under a great deal of stress due to personal matters—matters I would not get into for privacy reasons—and it had been easier for him to say he was working those late evening hours, where, in reality, he was having personal marriage difficulties at home. I assured them that he was not asked to work beyond his assigned hours. In fact, it was just the opposite—I had encouraged him to take care of his family and himself. It was challenging, but as a team we eventually recovered. High levels of morale were restored, but the memory of his tragic death lingered.

When times became hard, I often reminded myself that my difficulties did not even come close to the hardships and challenges my mother had experienced during the Jim Crow era, the racial, economic, educational, and social injustices, and the fight for basic civil rights, while at the same time raising four children on her own. Her strength and character provided me with the inspiration I needed to become the best version of myself. I embraced the *concept of being me.* Becoming the master chief afforded me the ability to lead, develop, and thrive, so I could do things my way. Just like she did. Making master chief epitomized my mother's struggle and the strength she demonstrated to provide a better life for me and my siblings, and that is something I did not dare take for granted.

Humbled by all of this, I found even greater strength in just being myself. I became even bolder, more courageous, and confident. I stopped concerning myself with things that did not matter. I worried even less about what others thought. I began to understand my purpose and value to others.

Now coming up on 20 years in the Navy, I had to determine my next career move. My older brother had always said to me, "don't do one day over 20 years." After 20 years of honorable service in the military, service members can retire and earn 50 percent of their basic pay.

Because I had spent the last four years overseas, I did not have much insight into the economic and employment environment in the United States. I also knew I did not want to retire in Japan. So, I accepted orders to the Office of Naval Intelligence in Suitland, Maryland.

I was also selected as a panel member on the Navy-wide Chief Petty Officer Selection Board in Millington, Tennessee, on a temporary assignment for several weeks. This was a great honor because I would now participate in the process of reviewing, selecting, and promoting the next round of chief petty officers as future leaders for the entire Navy.

CHAPTER 12

SELF-REFLECTION

Office of Naval Intelligence – Suitland
Maryland

"Knowing yourself is the beginning of all wisdom."
—**Aristotle**

I n August 2001, I reported to the Office of Naval Intelligence in
Suitland, Maryland, just seven miles outside of Washington D.C.
The Office of Naval Intelligence[28] is the military intelligence agency
of the United States Navy. Established in 1882, the Office of Naval
Intelligence is the oldest member of the United States intelligence
community and serves as the nation's premier source of maritime
intelligence. Since the First World War, its mission has broadened
to include real-time reporting on the developments and activities of
foreign navies, protecting maritime resources and interests, monitoring and countering transnational maritime threats, and providing

---

28 Office of Naval Intelligence. https://www.oni.navy.mil/.

technical, operational, and tactical support to the U.S. Navy and its partners, along with surveying the global maritime environment.

There I served as the Intelligence Communications Division's leading chief and senior enlisted advisor for the IT and Communications Directorate. I was thrilled to be back in the United States after two back-to-back tours of duty in Guam and Japan.

Office of Naval Intelligence headquaters building in Suitland, Maryland.

On a normal Tuesday morning, as I was just getting settled into my new position and role within the organization, the world changed right before my eyes.

That morning was September 11, 2001. Nineteen terrorists[29] tied to the Islamic extremist group al Qaeda hijacked four airplanes and carried out suicide attacks against targets in the United States. The twin towers of the World Trade Center in New York City and the Pentagon in Arlington, Virginia, were attacked, and one plane went down in a field in Shanksville, Pennsylvania. It was later dis-

---

29 September 11 attacks. https://www.history.com/topics/21st-century/9-11-attacks.

covered that the plane had been headed to the U.S. Capitol in Washington, D.C.

That morning I was sitting in my office, doing my regular work when one of the on-duty watch supervisors came in.

"Hey, master chief," he said, "a plane just flew into the World Trade Center."

We gathered round to watch the news coverage on the big screens, thinking then it had been a terrible, tragic accident that a plane had hit the North Tower. But then we saw the second airplane hit the South Tower. Suddenly, we understood that our nation was under attack.

I had dedicated my career to intelligence work, which was all about forecasting. We generally knew about things before they happened, and we worked to thwart them. But this was something we clearly did not know about. I was shaken to my core—we were not used to something that horrific happening without having any intelligence on it.

We immediately stood up a war room and put together our emergency incident response, situational awareness, and operational support requirements. At this point, the only real-time intel we had was from the news stations. It was surreal.

Soon we received word that another hijacked plane had crashed into the Pentagon, and then that the final one had crashed in Shanksville. As military professionals and leaders, we take an oath to support and defend our constitution against all enemies, foreign and domestic, and we all understood that the moment was *now*.

At that point, we did not know if there would be more planes.

We received a notification that all federal government buildings were being evacuated, including the White House, the U.S. Capitol, and other federal buildings in the Washington D.C. metropolitan area. Internally, I coordinated with the on-shift personnel and made sure they had all the instruction and guidance they needed. Then all non-essential personnel were told to leave the facility. That included me. So, I rushed to my car and headed home.

I lived in Alexandria, Virginia, which was about 13 miles and a 35-minute commute from Suitland, Maryland. But with all the federal buildings, landmarks and public facilities being evacuated, the entire Washington D.C. Metropolitan Area was flooded with traffic, chaos, and uncertainty.

Bumper-to-bumper traffic and jammed streets. I sat in my car for 30 minutes at a time with no movement. I could see the heavy, dark smoke billowing in the air from the Pentagon attack. As I crossed the 14th Street Bridge passing through D.C. into Arlington, the sky grew darker and darker. I could smell the thick, rancid jet fuel as I moved closer to the Pentagon. A trip that usually took 35 minutes stretched into three hours as I navigated hastily erected roadblocks and detours. I was grateful to have a full tank of gas.

Because so many people were trying to make calls, I could not get a cell signal to make a call myself. Thankfully, I could still tune into the radio to get a sense of what was going on. When I finally arrived home, I was transfixed by the news.

That is when the global war on terrorism began.

When I returned to work a couple days later, the mood of the organization was somber, but it was not slow. There was an undercurrent of intensity. We all wanted to do *something*.

So, I dug deeper into my work. I was just weeks into my new position within the Intelligence Communications Division, and I found there were some leadership challenges with respect to favoritism and lower standards of excellence than were expected, similar to those I had found in my days at the elephant cage at the Naval Security Group Department in Guam. The difference was that now I was the master chief, and the operational shifts that had to occur due to the terrorist attacks afforded the opportunity for immediate change. Additionally, the climate and work culture in the Washington D.C. area was vastly different from a small island over 8,000 miles away.

Yes, there were initial growing pains for the staff, but the transformation was immediate. The work culture, team morale, and a sense of professional excellence and pride were vastly improved. I had the full support and backing of a Navy captain, fellow master chief, and the direct support of the command master chief. In addition to my leading chief petty officer role within the division, I was also the senior enlisted advisor. I had a direct path to the captain who led and commanded our directorate, which expanded my influence to include more than 175 total personnel, to include a dozen or so chief petty officers.

Although I enjoyed my role as the senior enlisted advisor and my relationship with the captain, I was still the same old grumpy master chief with high standards. I was not going to lower my standards to meet other's expectations.

One afternoon, the chief warrant officer and I were set to brief the captain on our personnel rankings for the E-6s. In the Navy, rankings are an important tool to help determine who is most qualified for a promotion. That particular day, the captain was as cheerful as he always was when the chief warrant officer and I stepped into his office.

"Hey Warrant, hey Master Chief," he said. "Please have a seat."

We sat down at a small, beautifully made, circular Maplewood table. While the warrant opened the conversation, she deferred to me to present our list of rankings. I outlined our ranking process, and if I recall correctly, there were about 25 names listed in numerical order, accompanied by a stack of supporting documents. When I finished my briefing, I slowly slid the documents across the table for the captain's review and signature.

But as he looked at the documents, his face turned red. It took less than a few seconds for him to push the documents back over to me.

"Master Chief, I don't like this," he said, with disappointment in his tone.

"Well, sir, these are our rankings."

I pushed the documents back toward him, but I accidently pushed too hard. Suddenly, all the papers flew into the air and fell all over him and the floor. The warrant, horrified, jumped to pick up the papers, uttering quick apologies. The captain muttered something as I sat there quietly.

What the Hell did I just do? I thought to myself. To them, it looked like I was *very* firmly standing my ground. Little did they know I was in shock myself. This had been completely unintentional.

After the warrant and the captain restored the stack of documents and placed them back on the desk, the captain spoke.

"I think I will have to reassess and consider your viewpoint, Master Chief."

Once he had decided to listen, I then explained the Navy's Chief Selection Board process because the naval officer's promotion process is separate and different from that of enlisted. He understood my rationale for the rankings and accepted my explanation. Going in, I had known that the captain had a particular sailor in mind who he believed should have been ranked number one. If I remember correctly, she was ranked number four or five, so I figured he would have something to say about it. While I had always intended to hold my ground, I had not planned for a stack of papers to fly in the air at a senior officer who I genuinely enjoyed working with and very much respected. But that was the benefit of being a master chief—I could always stand by my principles and be objectively consistent without fear of retribution.

Later that advancement cycle, we learned that three or four of our ranked personnel were promoted to chief petty officer—the most in the history of our directorate. The candidate the captain favored was selected for promotion the following year.

Many leaders find it difficult to be completely honest and straightforward with their supervisors, employees, and even their friends. But throughout my Navy career, I worked to be forthright and consistent.

That really hit home for me when I took a philosophy course at Northern Virginia Community College and had to write an essay on Niccolò Machiavelli's, *The Prince*.[30] "It is a book of political philosophy that describes the perfect leader in a republic form of government, as we have in the U.S. today."

Machiavelli explains what qualities the ideal "prince" should have as well as how he should go about conducting his business. He asks, "Is it better to be loved than feared, or the reverse?" Although both qualities would be desirable, he argues that if the prince were to choose between being feared or loved by his people, the prince should choose fear. While living under fear is not ideal, it is true that the feared prince is a better leader than a loved prince. Love and fear are two completely different emotions that bring out the best and the worst in everyone. He tells us that a combination of the two would be the best, but that it is almost impossible to have both.

He concludes that, "Since men love at their own choice and fear at the prince's choice, a wise prince takes care to base himself on what is his own." In other words, a smart leader knows that if power is awarded based on love, power can be taken away just as easily if people fall out of love with you. But if people fear the prince, the power is held in his hands.[31]

Though I enjoyed Machiavelli's book and understood his philosophy, for my own purposes I exchanged the word "fear" with "respect." As a leader, I chose respect over love. Even today, I lead and manage by the principle of respect over both fear and love.

---

30 Niccolò Machiavelli: Fear or Love—540 Words | Bartleby.
31 https://www.bartleby.com/essay/Niccol%C3%B3-Machiavelli-Fear-or-Love-P3C75DEC8M6S.

Respect is clear and consistent, and I have found it to be the best approach for leaders of medium to large organizations. I used that leadership philosophy to guide the way I worked to improve the Intelligence Communications Division, and over a short period, the division's technical support vastly improved.

We implemented the Intelligence Communications Division Training/Qualification Program, the Professional Excellence Academy, the 100% Advancement Campaign, and the Chiefs Selection Board Seminars where morale and enthusiasm went through the roof. Although there were a few disgruntled personnel who had been realigned to other roles, they all did their jobs despite their lack of excitement for the constructive changes that had taken place.

Office of Naval Intelligence Professional Excellence Academy instructors.

In the summer of 2002, I was called to return to Naval Personnel Command, Millington, Tennessee for four weeks where I was chosen again as a panel member for the Navy-wide Chief Petty Officer

Selection Board. After making the selections for the next round of new Navy chiefs, I returned to Maryland. Upon my arrival, one of my closest fellow master chiefs informed me he had planned to submit his paperwork to retire from the Navy. We had a lot of responsibility between the two of us, and when I left for Tennessee, he had to balance his regular assignment along with filling in for me during my four-week absence.

"I'm tired man, I have to go," he said.

"No, you're just tired because I haven't been here," I told him.

He listened, at least for a while. But then I felt it as well. For years, I would hear others say how they knew when it was time to retire. Their responses were consistent, as they would all say, "Trust me, you would know, it's a feeling."

About three weeks after our conversation, I found myself in deep introspection. I reflected back on my entire career and life and now had to decide. I had been 17 years old when I joined the Navy. Now at 38, I looked back on a long, tough climb. I could stay in the Navy and enjoy the master chief status for nine more years or hang up my boots now. But I too, was tired, and I knew I had always wanted to retire at the 20-year mark. At this point, I was one year past my goal.

I thought back to the day I had spoken with my old basketball coach, Dr. Carlos Smith, when we had first discussed my joining the military. I reflected on these very words. "You could have a career, obtain an education, play basketball, travel the world, and serve our country," he said. And I had done it, all of it, and more, and even made master chief petty officer. And the fact that I could work my way up through the ranks from seaman recruit (E-1) to master chief (E-9), I figured I could do anything that I put my mind to. So, I called my mother and informed her that I was considering retiring from the Navy. She told me that she was very proud of me and supported my decision either way.

After a couple weeks of mulling it over, I decided to retire. I discussed it with my fellow master chief and captain and decided I would submit my retirement papers.

I reached out to the master chief and said, "Shipmate, I'm putting in my papers, I am going to retire. My time has come, I feel it."

He responded, "Really? Now you cannot talk me out of it, I going to submit my paperwork as well."

I later spoke with the captain, my paperwork/request in hand. "Captain, with the upmost respect, I would appreciate your consideration and approval of my request to retire from the U.S. Navy."

He looked at me and responded, "Master Chief, with all you've done for the Navy and these sailors, you deserve the right to retire on your own terms, and I support you." It was mid-September in 2002, and my retirement date was set for February 2003. I had five months remaining. My fellow master chief's retirement date was scheduled for a month later, in March 2003.

As I contemplated what I wanted to do after retirement, I considered two paths. One was the Troops to Teachers Program aimed at recruiting quality teachers for schools serving low-income families in an effort to relieve teacher shortages. I met all of the eligibility requirements for the program, and I had always been passionate about education. The other path was law school. I had my sights set on becoming a public defender to help advocate for others who did not have a voice.

I spoke with a former classmate of mine who then worked as a high school principal. He advised me against the Troops to Teachers Program.

"Kenneth, don't do it. These kids are so bad they would put the fire out in Hell," he said.

Having spent so many years in the military enforcing good order and discipline, I knew being in a classroom full of disruptive kids would be a potential recipe for disaster, given that my former classmate had described an environment where kids were not respecting authority. So, I placed all my energy and focus on getting into law school.

Then, while I was in the midst of transitioning from the Navy and focusing on getting into law school, all of a sudden, the D.C. sniper shootings were making the headlines.

The first time I had returned home after being away for six years, I had come back to a war on drugs, and Washington D.C. had become the murder capital of the U.S. This time, and while awaiting retirement, I returned to the 9/11 attacks, the war on terrorism, and now, the D.C. sniper. Washington D.C. was like another warzone. Many people, including myself at times, worried they could be the next casualty if they were at the wrong place at the wrong time.

The D.C. snipers were two men who carried out a series of random, coordinated shootings in October 2002 in the D.C. Metropolitan

Region, which includes the District of Columbia, Maryland, and Virginia. In total, 10 people were killed and three were wounded.

People were killed doing mundane, everyday things. It was senseless. An FBI analyst was killed while loading supplies she had picked up from Home Depot into her trunk. The night she was killed, I was near the scene at a Giant Supermarket. I was standing in line to pay for a few items when someone came inside the store shouting that there had been another shooting. I kept my cool and remained calm. As I walked out of the store, I saw several people walking in frantic zigzags. I could not help but laugh. It seemed so ridiculous to me at the time.

To get home, I had to turn left on to Route 7 in Alexandria. To see what was going on with the sniper situation, I had to turn right. So, being curious, I turned right, drove a few blocks, and discovered that the Virginia State Police had set up a checkpoint and roadblocks. All traffic was being diverted, and I had to make a U-turn and headed home. I even called a friend while I was driving to tell him about the shoppers walking in zigzags.

A couple of days later, I made a stop at an Exxon gas station to fill up the tank. The gas station was right around the corner from where I lived and on the same road, Route 7, as the Giant Supermarket near the Home Depot where the FBI analyst was killed. As I went to select the gas, I discovered the pump was not on or had malfunctioned.

I made several attempts to catch the attendant's attention by waving and yelling from a distance, but to no avail. I then walked towards the plexiglass booth where I could see the attendant standing with his back turned. He was actually on a cell phone carrying on an intense conversation. So, I stood there with my arms crossed, waiting to see how long it would take for him to notice I was there. I stood there for one minute, two minutes, and at about the third minute mark, feeling the annoyance and frustration build, it suddenly hit me that the DC snipers might have me in their sights *right now.*

I started to freaking panic, and dispensing of my tolerant patience, I began to frantically beat on the plexiglass window.

"The damn sniper could be out here!" I yelled, finally getting his attention to turn on the gas pump.

I began running back to my car, zigzagging the whole way. I hastily started the pump and laid as flat as I could in the car so the sniper could not potentially see me. My heart was racing, and I was in a panic. When the tank was full, I then peeped my head up to scan the scene before removing the pump. Just days earlier I had been making light of others for being spooked coming out of the grocery store, and now I was literally terrified. I remained on guard and alert for many days following that scare.

The two snipers, John Allen Muhammad and Lee Boyd Malvo, were finally captured and arrested October 24. Muhammad was sentenced to death and Malvo was sentenced to life in prison. While their reign of terror was relatively short, it was extremely deadly, and has left a lasting impression on me, the families of the victims, and those who lived in the Washington D.C. Metro Area during that time. Following these events, with all the violence and chaos that we had experienced in Washington D.C., I found myself walking in fear and reflecting on my future plans.

In time, I was able to refocus my attention on studying for the Law School Admissions Test (LSAT) and I prepared my admissions package for the University of South Carolina. On weekends, I took LSAT prep classes. As the November exam date inched closer, I gathered together my GPA, several letters of recommendation, and a personal letter that highlighted how I had served in Operation Southern Watch in the Persian Gulf and the global war on terrorism. Plus, I made it clear that I was a hometown kid from Cherry Street. The law school was just a mile or two from where I grew up. I thought I had a good chance of getting in.

In mid-November 2002, I took the LSAT exam. While awaiting the results, I reflected on my Navy career and experiences and the obstacles my mother faced growing up in the segrated south. My challenges in the U.S. Navy paled in comparison to what my mother and other African Americans endured in the Jim Crow era, i.e., institutionalized socio-economic discrimination, and particularly educational disparities. Many years later, I had the opportunity to leverage the Navy's tuition assistance program and the Montgomery G.I. Bill to pay for a college education.

The effects and negative impacts of the legacy of the educational history in South Carolina can still be felt today. In particular, the South Carolina Negro Act of 1740, which remained in effect until 1865, prohibited African Americans from growing their own food, learning to read, moving freely, assembling in groups, or earning money. This 1740 Act prohibition of learning to read directly impacted my family, specifically my mother's grandparents, her mother and father, as it did all of the African Americans living in the state of South Carolina at the time.

Personally, I wanted the opportunity to exercise my passion to help people grow and understand their great opportunities. I thought about how I myself had been an involuntary participant in the Scared Straight Program when I was in middle school, simply because of my zip code and being considered an at-risk youth. What if there were a "Scared *Smart* Program" for at-risk youth? Education is the solution. I think the school boards of the cities and counties of South Carolina should focus their efforts and investment on educating at-risk youth and scaring them in to being smart, versus having law enforcement and prisoners scaring the youth into not making bad choices.

My vision of becoming a public defender was because I wanted to help and provide alternative life choices to young adults who faced similar circumstances to those that I had, as well be a voice and hope for others. The history and legacy of my mother's experience inspired me and gave me the energy and fortitude to ignore the naysayers and those who placed barriers and obtacles in my way. When I felt a challenge and became frustrated with military life, whether due to conflicts with others, working conditions on ships, failures or mistakes, I would just reflect on my mother's experiences and I would almost instantly pull myself out of it.

It was, in general, a time for self-reflection, but that would have to wait. I still had to officially retire from the Navy.

I didn't want to have a retirement ceremony or anything special because my mother could not travel to Maryland. At that point, she was in a wheelchair and paralyzed on her right side. She could get around with her walker, but a big trip like that would have been too much for her.

However, my captain and fellow master chief insisted, and the ceremony ended up being emotional for me. As I sat there, taking it all in, I felt like I hadn't slept for 36 hours. I had served for 21-and-a-half years, and it was all ending that day. I'd been through so much to get there. It was overwhelming. I had come a long way from Cherry Street—and my mother was proud of how far I'd come.

Me leading the Office of Naval Intelligence (ONI-4) Department during an inspection.

The reception included cake-cutting, gift giving, and an emotional farewell. It was clearly the end of a chapter in my life. I left the Office of Naval Intelligence for the last time on January 28, 2003. I was escorted to my car and drove off for the final time, "Shipmate going Ashore." As I drove through Maryland, D.C. and passed the Washington Monument and the Pentagon, and on to Alexandria, the stress, responsibility, and anxiety that had long been constant companions began to fade.

It was the beginning of a new and fresh start. The next morning when I awoke, I felt refreshed, renewed, and generally happy as I waited the results from my LSAT and notification from the University of South Carolina Law School. In the meantime, I applied and interviewed for a couple defense contractor jobs as a back-up plan. I figured it never hurt to be too prepared.

In mid-February, I received a notification letter stating that my application to the University of South Carolina law school was denied. Despite having what I considered an outstanding admissions package highlighting my military experiences, GPA scores, letters of recommendation and a personal letter, I was informed that my LSAT score was not high enough and was below the targeted percentile.

Here are some excerpts from my personal letter, written nearly 18 years ago. I have learned and accomplished a lot since that time. My goal was to become a public defender to be an advocate and voice for those who struggle to speak for themselves:

> *School of Law University of South Carolina Admissions Committee,*
>
> *In view of my personal, professional, and academic history, I recognize the the importance of this personal statement to you, the Admissions Committee. My statement will not only detail specifics, but it will represent my only voice in an attempt to persuade you of my strong desire for admission to the University of South Carolina's School of Law. It will also highlight my commitment towards the successful completion of law school and future contributions to the state of South Carolina.*

At age 17, I graduated from W.J. Keenan High School in Columbia (1981), joined the U.S. Navy and dedicated over 21 years of honorable service to the country. During my high school years, I didn't clearly understand the value of a good education. Though those weren't the best of times growing up in a single-parent household, I did understand the value of hard work and dedication. Because of that understanding, I was able to achieve the highest enlisted paygrade and hold the title of master chief petty officer, one of the most distinguished and well-respected positions in the U.S. Navy. Also, I served in the Persian Gulf during Operation Desert Shield/Southern Watch, served onboard two naval ships, and on several overseas and remote assignments, where I received numerous personal awards and commendations. The hard work and dedication paid off. Fortunately, I then learned the value of a good education; I went on to earn an Associate of Science and Bachelor's of Science Degree. I graduated magna cum laude and was selected for the Who's Who in American Junior Colleges. I was elected as the vice president, Phi Theta Kappa, Tau Nu Chapter, and served as the education service officer onboard a ship of 410 naval personnel. Academically, I had to work even harder considering that I was leading and managing up to 125 personnel. I have served in a variety of positions and have devoted numerous hours to the community. I enjoy mentoring and counseling sailors, and giving assistance to the less fortunate.

My desire to attend the University of South Carolina School of Law is a very personal one due to several reasons. Primarily, South Carolina is the home state where I was born and raised, and I have a strong desire to make a difference in both the classroom and community. I have learned the values of education, dedication, hard work, and commitment to excellence. I recognize that I can make a difference in the lives of the people around me. I also possess strong leadership skills and abilities—I work well with others, and have outstanding oral presentation skills. In view of my LSAT scores, I am even more determined to work harder, and not only successfully complete law school, but also to be among the top students! And to go on to serve the citizens of the state of South Carolina. I believe I am the type of individual that your committee would seek to have in a law school classroom. In closing, my contributions to the law school would be boundless; the adversity and diversity of my upbringing, the exposure to other countries, cultures, and naval personnel nationwide has afforded me access to a multitude of both professional and personal enlightenment opportunities which will translate into an excellent benefit to the University of South Carolina School of Law.

Even today, I still have a bit of a chip on my shoulder about not being accepted, particularly when I reflect on the history of the state and I how I really had a passion to make a difference. It's clear that the University of South Carolina Law School placed an inordinate weight on test scores versus all other qualifications, which tends to put candidates who have had a less than rigorous education at a disadvantage. There are now top law schools, to include Harvard, Georgetown, Northwestern University, and William and Mary, the oldest law school,[32] that do not include the LSAT as an admission requirement for a number of good reasons. This has had a direct and positive influence on diversity in American law

---

32 The LSAT is No Longer Required at These and Other Law Schools: Why Law Schools Are Ditching the LSAT | LawCrossing.com.

schools and the eventual practice of law throughout the country, if not the world.

I informed my mother and friends in South Carolina.

Later, I called my mother and had a discussion about moving home, back to South Carolina. I wanted badly to be there for her and to make a difference in the town I grew up in. But she told me I should not.

"Son, I would love for you to come home, but there is nothing here," she said.

In response, I stated, "But you are there, Mom."

"Yes, I am, Kenneth, but I'm old and you have to live your life. You have a lot going for yourself and you need to continue on that path."

Though disappointed, she positively encouraged me to use my cryptologic and Navy experience to do something else with my life. I spent a lot of time reflecting on my future and how I could best leverage my military experience, education, and experise. I was still frustrated by not being admitted to law school.

Only a few days later, I received a job offer from a large defense contractor and accepted a position as project manager supporting enterprise information technology initiatives at the Defense Information Systems Agency (DISA) in Arlington, Virginia. Eventually, I applied for a masters of science program at George Mason University in Fairfax, Virginia and was accepted. Interestingly, despite only having a general education diploma, I always knew my mother had this innate wisdom that was indisputable. I enjoyed our conversations and would ask her questions with the anticipation of knowing I was going to receive an unvarnished response filled with insight, perspective, discernment, and love. Given the path and journey that I continue on even today, it is clear she gave me sage advice.

CHAPTER 13

TRANSITION

Defense Information
Systems Agency – Arlington, Virginia

"Any transition is easier if you believe in yourself and your talent."
—**Priyanka Chopra**

I t was March 2003, and I had started my first civilian job as a
defense contractor at the Defense Information Systems Agency
(DISA) on South Courthouse Road in Arlington, Virginia.

DISA's primary mission is to provide information technology and
communications support to the president, vice president, secre-
tary of defense, the military services, the combatant commands,
and any system contributing to the defense of the United States.
DISA also provides direct support to U.S. Cyber Command's cyber operations mission, by providing innovative technology, operational structures and processes, and doctrinal concepts for command, control, and leadership that enhance the government's

capabilities to respond to dynamic and hostile threats to the nation. I commonly referred to DISA as the telecommunications and telephone company for the Department of Defense. DISA has a storied history of accomplishment dating back to the 1960s when it was known as the Defense Communications Agency (DCA).

701 South Courthouse Road, Arlington, Virginia, Defense Information Systems Agency (DISA) former headquarters building. Now the Naval Suppot Activitiy.

The DISA headquarters building was just a three-minute drive from the Pentagon. The airplane that attacked the Pentagon on 9/11 literally flew over the facility in which I was now working. I saw that side of the Pentagon, now a memorial, on a daily basis.

Similar to the Commander, Naval Security Group, the DISA headquarters has since relocated to Fort George G. Meade, Maryland, home to the National Security Agency (NSA).

The global war on terrorism was in high gear and the impact of the 9/11 attacks continued to affect our country and how we worked and lived our lives. For me, this was a time of transition.

Transitioning out of the military can be difficult for many people. According to a survey conducted by the Pew Research Center in December 2011,[33] about 27 percent of veterans who have served in the armed forces have a hard time re-entering civilian life. That number grows to 44 percent among veterans who have served in the decade since the September 11 terrorist attacks. The study shows that veterans who had graduated from college had an easier time readjusting to their post-military life than veterans who were just high school graduates. In addition, veterans who had had emotionally traumatic experiences while serving or had suffered serious injuries also had a more difficult time adjusting.

It can be a shock to the system when you come out of the military and realize regular civilians do not generally care or respect your service—especially when you have spent a significant part of your life relying on Navy camaraderie or come from the Marines where they will never leave anyone on the battlefield.

Personally, I felt relieved. I almost felt a sense of freedom. Dealing with that level of responsibility on a daily basis can be exhausting.

I had spent 21-and-a-half years serving in the U.S. Navy. Each day I had showed up wearing my uniform ready for duty. Now, I was a civilian contractor wearing a suit and tie. That part was relatively

---

33 The Difficult Transition from Military to Civilian Life | Pew Research Center https://www.pewresearch.org/social-trends/2011/12/08/the-difficult-transition-from-military-to-civilian-life/

easy as I was accustomed to keeping my military uniform squared away, with high grooming standards, and yes, shining my shoes.

There was a Today's Man clothing store nearby where I stocked up on the latest suits, shirts, and ties. It was exciting. I was 39, single, and working in a job where I did not have supervisory responsibilities. I had more time to focus on honing my technical skills and continuing my education.

I applied for and was accepted at the George Mason University School of Engineering Master's program. That acceptance letter was gratifying after not having been admitted into the University of South Carolina Law School.

Even today, I still feel a sense of disappointment at not having been admitted to the University of South Carolina Law School. Although there have been significant changes since the Jim Crow era and my days growing up on Cherry Street, South Carolina continues to lag behind other more progressive states with respect to its legacy of exclusion and racial inequality. I must acknowledge times are better but there is more work and healing ahead.

Bear in mind, the Civil War essentially started in South Carolina. The event that triggered the war occurred at Fort Sumter in Charleston, South Carolina on April 12, 1861. Claiming this fort as their own, the Confederate Army opened fire on the federal garrison and forced it to lower the American flag in surrender. Lincoln called out the militia to suppress this insurrection. This was the beginning of the Civil War where abolishing slavery was the central issue. When I reflect on my own disappointment, I wonder if it was a signal or a reminder of my mother's warning of, "There's nothing here." It was through her encouragement that

I remained in D.C. because there was nothing for me in South Carolina.

I continued to enjoy the work of being a defense contractor and the salary was great. I was contributing to the mission as I primarily worked in a non-supervisory technical role. I did not have much authority or influence—instead, I was responsible for accomplishing a task or set of operations, or a deliverable outlined in a contract or statement of work.

As a retired master chief, I appreciated the break from responsibility, but I did struggle with the change in authority level the role brought. I was used to leading, managing, and directing others to ensure a smooth operation. There were plenty of instances when the old adage "the customer is always right" was far from true, even when the federal government was the customer. Eventually, I concluded that while I enjoyed the work, being in the role of a contractor was not an ideal fit for me. I recognized, given my background and experience, that I needed to be in a leadership role. If one old adage turned out to be wrong, maybe another would turn out to be right, if you cannot beat them, join them.

So, I applied for a federal government position at DISA supporting the Mission Assurance, Continuity of Operations, and their Critical Infrastructure Protection Program. I interviewed with a gentleman who would eventually become my first mentor within the federal government.

As I arrived for our interview, I was a bit nervous. After all, I had spent 21 years in the military, and had little experience at job interviewing.

When he welcomed me into his office, he was excited.

"Hey Shipmate, please have a seat," he said.

I was initially taken aback because "shipmate" is a Navy term used to indicate camaraderie. So, it was clear to me that he was probably a Navy veteran. I was instantly at ease.

He outlined the job description and explained the position requirements. He then asked me to tell him about my background and experience. After that one question, he talked non-stop for the remainder of the interview about the job and life working at DISA. He told me that he had served in the U.S. Navy and was a retired chief warrant officer but was once a senior chief petty officer, which explained the shipmate greeting.

When I left the interview, though he was kind and I liked his positive energy and enthusiasm, I did not know if I would be selected for the job. He had only asked me to tell him about myself but never asked any additional interview questions. For weeks, I did not hear anything. However, I eventually received a call and an official offer for the position, which I happily accepted.

Just as in the U.S. Military, federal civilian employees take a solemn oath to support and defend the constitution against all enemies, foreign and domestic. I was unaware of this requirement until I attended orientation for my new job and the entire group had to stand and take the oath. I did so gladly, as I had done the four times I had enlisted and re-enlisted over my 21-year naval career.

During the first week in the office, my supervisor outlined my roles and responsibilities, including the technical oversight of contractor functions. Additionally, I was the information systems security officer and the administrator for classified systems within our division. I now had authority, I genuinely enjoyed working for my boss, and the team dynamics were great.

As I became more comfortable in my new role, I eventually asked my boss the question that had been in the back of my mind ever since he had interviewed me.

"During the interview, you only asked me one question. Why only one question?"

He looked at me and smiled.

"Well, when I saw your resume and the accomplishments you had achieved over your Navy career, particularly the fact that you were a retired master chief, and also that you had later been a contractor for DISA, I knew you were the person for the job! But the federal government has an established process with specific guidelines on recruitment and hiring, which includes the interview process," he said.

He told me only a few candidates had qualified for the position, but once I entered his office and fully answered the question, he did not feel he had to go any further because the remaining questions were basic technical and occupational requirements that were clearly demonstrated by my work experience.

Later, my boss was reassigned to the lead our agency's Base Realignment and Closure (BRAC) initiative, which was the Department of Defense's effort to reduce the number of military bases and save taxpayer dollars by relocation to Fort Meade, Maryland. As a result, our entire team was reorganized to another internal division. The morale of the division shifted downward with the organizational changes due to the relocation. It was a time of uncertainty for all.

Like many other employees at DISA, including my boss, I did not want to move to Maryland or make a three-hour-a-day commute from Alexandria to Fort Meade. I began to seek other employment opportunities within a closer commuting distance.

In August 2007, I enrolled in the last two classes I needed to obtain my master of science degree. I was also dating a wonderful young lady and having a great time. Things were going well, and I was excited about life.

But in September, my mother's health took a turn for the worse. I had made several trips to Columbia to visit her, and it was a painful experience. Eventually, I received a call from my sister informing me that our mother was not doing well, and that I should come home.

I returned to Columbia and visited her again in the hospital. She was on a respirator and could not speak, and was laying there with her eyes open. We knew she did not have long.

I could not handle seeing my mother in that condition. It was too painful. I asked my siblings for their blessing and support to leave.

"I can't sit here and watch Mom die," I told them. "I don't have the strength, and I don't have the courage."

They understood. I provided her doctor with my contact information and asked him to keep me posted on her condition and to please advise me of any significant changes. I then drove back to Alexandria, Virginia.

Three days later, the doctor called. He informed me he did not think she was going to make it, and that I should return as soon as possible. By the time I arrived back in Columbia, she had passed away.

My sister, brother, and I all worked together in planning the memorial and burial arrangements. I was grateful for how well we came together during this difficult time. My mother's funeral was beautiful. The pastor knew my mother well and he did a wonderful job eulogizing her and paying tribute to her life. Many of our relatives, her friends and colleagues came and paid their respects to this magnificent person who gave of herself to others. She was laid to rest at Greenlawn Memorial Park, which is less than a one-mile walk from the Veterans Hospital she retired from after 40 years of supporting military service members.

My mother was strong and fearless. She remains my hero and she is the inspiration behind me writing this book, to give back what was given to me, the legacy of her character.

That has been the constant thread that has carried me through all the difficulties and challenges in my life. My mother taught me about life and was the shining example of what character and integrity exemplify, to always be honest, to hold yourself accountable, to be dependable, to be respectful of others, to be yourself, to work hard and to never give up.

Charles de Gaulle, a former French army officer and statesman who led Free France against Nazi Germany in World War II, is quoted as saying, "A man of character finds a special attractiveness in difficulty, since it is only by coming to grips with difficulty that he can realize his potential."[34]

In December 2007, I completed all my coursework and graduated from George Mason University with a master's degree. Nonetheless, I continued to struggle with the loss of my mother.

She had proudly displayed my associate's and bachelor's degree certificates. Prior to her passing away, I had removed the two certificates from her living room, and then told her that I would pursue an even higher-level education, and that I was going to earn a master's degree because of the inspiration, encouragement, and wisdom she had provided throughout my youth and adulthood. Though she did not live to see me get that third degree, I did it all to honor her.

At this point, as I continued to grieve the loss of my mother, I knew I needed a shift in my career and life in general. The global war on terrorism remained a top priority for the nation, and I missed being part of the intelligence community. Leveraging my knowledge, skills, and abilities in my current role and my previous experience as a cryptologic technician, I applied for new position at the Defense Intelligence Agency (DIA). Only three weeks after applying, I was contacted for an interview. The interview process included sessions with two separate panels, the second was to be with two very senior intelligence personnel with information technology backgrounds. This was vastly different from the interview process at DISA. In addition, employment was conditional upon passing drug screening and a polygraph examination, commonly referred to as a lie detector test, and involved an extensive security

---

34 https://www.goodnewsnetwork.org/charles-de-gaulle-quote-on-difficulty/

clearance background investigation. In July 2008, I was selected for the position at the DIA. The DIA is an intelligence agency of the U.S. Federal Government, specializing in defense and military intelligence, and is a component of the Department of Defense (DoD) and the United States intelligence community but is a separate and distinct organization from the CIA.

Defense Intelligence Agency (DIA) Headquarters Joint Base Anacostia–Bolling in Washington, D.C

Following a three-day orientation at the DIA headquarters located on the premises of Joint Base Anacostia–Bolling in Washington, D.C., I was assigned to the Defense Intelligence Mission Area (DIMA) Portfolio Management Office, supporting the undersecretary of defense for intelligence, the highest-ranking intelligence official at the Pentagon, in a new role as the executive agent for managing intelligence mission information technology requirements.

I was excited to get back into the action and to have a change of pace. The commute to my new regular work location was only about a 15-minute drive from where I lived in Alexandria, Virginia. The work was challenging but exciting, and I relished the opportunity of collaborating with most of the intelligence agencies that had a defense or war mission. It was an experience like no other I had had up until that point in my career. I grew to learn and better understand how all the intelligence agencies worked together to protect our country and provide our warfighters, special operations forces, and other intelligence operatives with the support and capabilities they needed to perform their important sensitive missions and objectives around the world.

After a year and a half of working at the DIA, I found the perfect opportunity for a promotion within the Office of the Director of National Intelligence (ODNI) supporting the program manager, information sharing environment (PM-ISE), a department whose mission was directly aligned with enhancing the war on terrorism. The PM-ISE had been established by the Intelligence Reform and Terrorism Prevention Act, as a direct result of the 9/11 Commission recommendations to ensure intelligence information sharing across law enforcement, defense, and intelligence personnel, and to promote partnerships across federal, state, local, and tribal governments, the private sector, and international partners. I performed various organizational, technical, and administrative duties including the development of technical policies and guidance for intelligence sharing, and prepared congressional briefing books for high-level meetings, visits, and testimony regarding intelligence and information sharing and other related legislative matters. My direct supervisor was a relatively young senior executive and former Capitol Hill staffer on the U.S. House of Representatives Homeland Security and Government Affairs Committee.

This was particularly important work as the 9/11 Commission Report had outlined missed opportunities and gaps between the intelligence agencies, chiefly the FBI and CIA, that could have potentially thwarted the 9/11 attacks on our nation. It was a lot of work to facilitate communications and collaboration across these multiple entities. Given my experience of working with multiple intelligence agencies, to support better intelligence and information sharing was an ideal fit for me. I worked in a downtown D.C. office building that was managed and secured by the U.S. Department of State. It was a great location and was in close proximity of the White House. I recall on many occasions when we would regularly hear the presidential motorcade, 40 to 50 vehicles, including D.C. Police motorcycles, Secret Service SUVs, and other emergency and support vehicles. The sounds were loud, like rolling thunder and we would run to the windows when we heard the distinctive reverberations. This was a constant reminder of our important role in keeping America safe. I worked in that building during both the George W. Bush and Barack Obama administrations.

U.S. Presidential Motorcade – Washington D.C.

Despite the hard work and fast-paced challenges during that time, I enjoyed supporting our mission, particularly, the director of our organization, who was a former U.S. Ambassador to Colombia. During his career, he had served as a U.S. Foreign Service officer and a diplomat, stationed in various countries around the world. He was also appointed to the United States National Security Council as director of counterterrorism and counter-narcotics. After a distinguished career, he retired from government service but returned to the federal government following the September 11 attacks. He also was the third recipient of the National Intelligence Distinguished Public Service Medal, the highest award granted to non-career federal employees, private citizens or others who have performed distinguished service of exceptional significance for the United States intelligence community.

One day, when we were in his office, he shared a true story about Pablo Escobar, the Colombian drug lord and narco-terrorist who was the founder and leader of the Medellín Cartel.

The Medellín Cartel distributed powder cocaine and established the first smuggling routes into the United States. Escobar's infiltration into the U.S. created exponential demand for cocaine and by the 1980s it was estimated that Escobar sent monthly shipments of 70 to 80 tons of cocaine into the country from Colombia. As a result, he quickly became one of the richest people in the world, but consistently battled rival cartels domestically and abroad, leading to massacres and the murders of police officers, judges, locals, and prominent politicians, thereby making Colombia the murder capital of the world. Escobar is still the wealthiest criminal in history, having amassed an estimated net worth of $30 billion dollars by the time of his death. The ambassador laughed as he told me he had learned that when interrogators asked Pablo Escobar why he ultimately surrendered and turned himself in to authorities, he cited the relentless pursuit by the head of the Colombian security service and that "hijo de puta ambassador." Translating that from Spanish to English, he referred to the ambassador of Colombia as a "son of a bitch." Those were strong words coming from this notorious drug lord. And that was but one of the ambassador's great and legendary stories of his many years as a diplomat.

Though I enjoyed his story about Pablo Escobar, he shared with me an even more courageous and personal story about his time as a Freedom Rider. As a young man he challenged racial laws in the South in the 1960s, refusing to abide by the laws designating that seating on buses be segregated by race. Of particular significance to this story, the ambassador was not African American, and this was during the times of major racial strife and segregation in the South. In fact, there were many races and voices that stood against inequality and for equal rights for all Americans during those difficult times. Having grown up in the 1960s, his courage held a special meaning to me personally. His integrity and respect for others are important values that had been instilled in me as a child.

Even to this day, the former ambassador remains one of the best people I have ever had the opportunity to work with or meet in my entire career. Though he was quite the statesman, when I think of him, I recall his cheerful personality. He really enjoyed Restaurant Week in D.C., when the restaurants would discount their prices and you could eat wonderful meals every day at very reasonable prices. The ambassador would become filled with excitement when each day of that week he would ask, "What are we having for lunch today?" Our office staff was relatively small, and it made for good fun, teambuilding, and a nice break given the intense nature of our environment. The ambassador was overall a good man and an exceptional human being.

Though my assignment there was relatively brief, I made an important contribution to the mission and learned a great deal. Afterwards, although I remained within the ODNI, I transitioned to another mission area, the Office of the National Counterintelligence Executive, now called the National Counterintelligence and Security Center. I was about to enter the human intelligence spy world.

CHAPTER 14

PEACE OF MIND

Human Intelligence (HUMINT)
Spy World – Washington, D.C.

"If you want peace of mind, stop fighting with your thoughts."
—Anonymous

"Welcome to the spy world, Mr. Earl."

After six years as a government official supporting U.S. Department of Defense communications and intelligence operations, terrorist intelligence information sharing, and a long career in the Naval Security Group protecting special intelligence systems and providing real-time sensitive cryptologic and signals intelligence operations support, I had now entered the field of human intelligence—working with spy-world greybeards.

In 2009, I was selected for a government position as a staff cyber action officer in the Office of the National Counterintelligence Executive (ONCIX), a mission area under the Office of the Director of National Intelligence. ONCIX was established to carry out counterintelligence, espionage, and security responsibilities for the Director of National Intelligence (DNI). The DNI sits at cabinet level and is the top intelligence official in the United States government. They oversee the National Intelligence Program and the U.S. intelligence community, which consists of 16 civilian and military organizations including the CIA, DIA, FBI, NSA, and other agencies.

Intelligence Community Campus-Bethesda 2017.

I recall my first day in the office, which was located on a highly secured classified floor in a nondescript office building within the Washington D.C. Metro Area. To access the building, operations, and information, all employees and contractors were required to have the highest level of government security clearance, pass a polygraph examination, and be read into special access programs. From the outside looking in, you never would have suspected that the most sensitive counterintelligence, counterespionage, and spy activities were being coordinated within this office building.

As I sat in the lobby area waiting for my sponsor to arrive, I marveled over the "Wall of Shame" that displayed a collection of photos, spy tradecraft, artifacts, and other information detailing America's history of espionage.

According to the Office of the Director of National Intelligence, the Wall of Shame was started in 2004 when the founder of the International Spy Museum and a former CIA officer donated materials. The Wall of Shame did just that—named and shamed American and foreign spies discovered after the 1930s. In 2017, the National Counterintelligence and Security Center broadened its vision to document and display the United States' history of espionage and sabotage according to museum standards. In September 2019, the project was renamed the Wall of Spies Experience, and it now showcases more than 200 spy stories from the origins of the U.S. to contemporary times.

The central exhibit, according to the Office of the Director of National Intelligence (ODNI), details the stories of more than 135 American spies who betrayed the country from time of the Revolutionary War to the 21st Century.

The John Jay Wall, for example, is named after one of America's founding fathers, who helped draft the Federalist Papers and served as the second governor of New York and the first chief justice of the United States. Jay also led the first significant American counterintelligence operation and was responsible for revealing a British scheme to kidnap or kill General George Washington.

The museum also features a Soviet Wall of Shame, commemorating six high-ranking Soviets who spied for the West during the

Cold War. Although the U.S. considers those spies to be heroes, all but one was caught and executed by the Soviet Union.

Beyond the stories of the people behind the espionage, the museum showcases the gadgets spies have used throughout history, including 39 Cold War-era concealment devices.

Mugshot of DIA's Ana Montes.

One name stood out to me more than the others, Ana Montes. In 1984, according to the FBI, Montes worked as a clerk at the Department of Justice in Washington. She openly spoke out about the U.S. government's policies toward Central America. Her beliefs attracted the attention of Cuban agents who suspected she would be sympathetic to their cause. They arranged a meeting and soon she agreed to help Cuba. By 1985, she was a full-blown spy. After working at the Department of Justice, she was employed by the Defense Intelligence Agency (DIA) for years, where she continued to work as a spy. Though security officials were concerned about her foreign policy views, they did not suspect her of spying.

She would memorize details in various files and type up the information at home to avoid detection. Then she would transfer the information onto encrypted disks, meet with her Cuban handler, and hand over the information.

She was caught thanks to a mix of gut feeling and undercover work. A DIA colleague sensed she was working with Cuban intelligence. That colleague reported her to a security official in 1996, and although she was investigated and interviewed, nothing happened. There was not enough evidence, at least not yet. Four years later, an undercover FBI agent received intel that an unidentified Cuban agent was working in Washington. That same security officer connected the dots, and the FBI opened an investigation. She was eventually arrested, and she admitted to revealing the identities of four undercover American intelligence officers working in Cuba. She pled guilty in 2002 and was sentenced to 25 years in prison, according to the FBI.

Montes never accepted any payment for stealing classified information beyond reimbursement for the expenses she incurred. She was motivated by ideology rather than money. She disagreed with U.S. foreign policy, so she took matters into her own hands.

The Wall of Spies Experience is quite different from the National Cryptologic Museum, which is open to the general public and takes you through the history of American cryptology—and which also displays collection of cryptographic equipment and techniques. Although the Wall of Spies Experience is not physically open to the public, one can get a sense of the stories it preserves at the INTEL.gov website.[35]

35 THE WALL OF SPIES EXPERIENCE: The Evolution of Espionage in America. https://www.intelligence.gov/wall-of-spies.

I was captivated by the maze of intrigue, mystery, and deception in this new world. It was all so different from my experience with the Navy. While I started to get excited about the job, I did think to myself, *What the Hell have I gotten myself into?*

Seeing all of this set the tone for what would lay ahead for me. Before long, my sponsor entered the lobby area and took me on a brief tour of the organization.

"Hi Mr. Earl, are you ready to get started?" she asked.

"Absolutely," I responded.

As we walked around the floor, the office felt sterile and cold. I did not see many people initially, but those I did see were quiet and intensely focused. It was nothing like the typical bustling operations center I had grown accustomed to. The floor was full of small offices and semi-private cubicle spaces. There were not many offices or desks decorated with photographs of families or personalized items. Before being assigned an office, I sat temporarily in one of those cubicles.

Even the offices were relatively sparse. My office had a desk, a single landline telephone, and a tall, leather executive chair. Each office had a long, glass window that stretched the length of the office and had a door for privacy.

I was assigned to the Strategy and Policy Division where I was responsible for providing cybersecurity and technical expertise and advice to support the counterintelligence mission and strategy.

Back then, there was an exponential growth and use of the internet and other technological capabilities that were transforming the use of traditional spy tradecraft. Foreign spies, criminal organizations, insider threat actors, and other nefarious characters were stealing sensitive government secrets, operational plans, and private information from computer networks for economic, military, political, and other illicit reasons by exploiting internet system vulnerabilities and susceptible people without even having to step foot in our country, government facilities, homes, or businesses.

The use of traditional spy tradecraft such as dead drops were also changing. A dead drop is a method of espionage tradecraft used to pass items or information between two individuals (e.g., a case officer and an agent, or two agents) using a secret location. This prearranged secret spot is the location where the espionage agent can leave messages, cash, documents, and other items, with the purpose of evading detection. By avoiding direct meetings, individuals can maintain operational security. This method contrasts with the live drop, so-called because two persons meet live to exchange items or information.

An example of a failed dead drop that was uncovered by Russia involved a fake rock. In 2006, the United Kingdom used a fake rock as a dead drop position to spy on Russia. Russian state television broadcasted a film claiming that British agents had hidden a sophisticated transmitter inside a fake rock left on a Moscow street. It accused embassy officials of allegedly downloading classified data from the transmitter using palm-top computers. The TV report showed a video of a man slowing his pace and glancing down at the rock before walking quickly away; another man was shown kicking the rock, while another walked by and picked it up. The Russian Federal Security Service (FSB) broadcasted X-rays of a hollowed-out rock filled with circuitry and accused four British men and one Russian of using it to download information.

Because of the internet and the speed of how data and information is exchanged and obtained, dead drops had now gone high-tech, as had our daily lives, and even the way human spies were recruited and how clandestine activities were conducted had also changed drastically. All of a sudden, we were dealing with social media, the exploitation of computer networks, USB devices, wireless and mobile devices, encryption, and more. Sure, we could use these new methods to our advantage. But so could the bad guys, whether they were nation state actors, criminals, hackers, or even the everyday citizen.

My job was to provide cyber expertise to the team, which was an ideal fit given my background and experience. Among my division's objectives was the development of classified and unclassified plans, policies, and strategies to detect, deter, and mitigate adversarial and insider threats. I had always considered my job to be exciting, but this was different. Every day I learned something that was intriguing, if not eye-opening. Sometimes it was downright scary, especially when I began to work more directly with the greybeards.

After several months in my new role, I was assigned to lead classified counterintelligence and cyber risk assessments. I was the lead government official on a team largely made up of retired high-level Senior Executive Service and Senior Executive Intelligence Service officials, who were now government contractors and consultants for the Office of the National Counterintelligence Executive. Each member typically had more than 25 years of counterespionage and special agent experience from one or more of the intelligence agencies, i.e., the CIA, FBI, Naval Criminal Investigative Service, Army Military Intelligence, and Air Force Office of Special Investigations, Basically, they were experienced spycatchers.

One of the greybeards I considered my covert mentor. I will call him Mr. G. Mr. G. was a consultant, a retired senior executive intelligence service officer, and a former member of the CIA's National Clandestine Service, the agency's elite team of spies. He told me stories of life as a career CIA intelligence and case officer who ran spy, human asset, and intelligence networks. In this new phase of my career, I often felt like I had a front row seat to a spy movie, but this was especially true when I worked with Mr. G., and I often felt like I needed to pinch myself in the middle of our conversations. Sometimes it all seemed like a dream.

Through our conversations, I started to understand what gave people the reasons or motivations to turn against their country and how they could be exploited. Those motivations included, but were not limited to finances, ideology, anger, revenge, sex and even blackmail. Mr. G explained how a good case officer can spot, assess, and develop a human asset based on those factors. I recall a story he shared one day, though I cannot disclose the details, the story was mind-blowing. He detailed how he surreptitiously conducted an operation using spy tradecraft that would not have appeared to be nefarious to an outsider. I followed up with a question.

"Mr. G., is it difficult to recruit in these foreign countries despite these motivations?" I asked.

He responded, "It depends, Kenneth, on what you mean by difficult. But I will tell you that it requires special skill, training, experience, and extreme caution. Please understand that these are not casual operations or undertakings. They are sensitive and quite dangerous. Generally, money and ideology are the main influencers, and yes, assessing and recruiting assets is extraordinarily complex."

"Can you give me an example?" I asked.

"[European country, not named] is a strategic location for international spy networks because of its geographic vicinity to the U.S. and other global interests. Recruitment in this country has the high potential for double-agent operations and other complexities that create challenges to our diplomatic and national security objectives."

"I think you answered my question, Mr. G. That sounds difficult to me. You should write a book," I said.

Because of Mr. G., I learned that the business of espionage was a dirty game, from false flag operations, concealment devices, safe houses, dead drops, to cyber spying—it is a full-on production of denial and deception. And to play in the spy world, you had to be at the top of your game.

Mr. G. was at the top of his. I also considered him to be quite the gentleman. A tall man, he stood about 6'2 or 6'3 and carried himself like a statesman. He typically wore a navy-blue suit and a crisp white shirt and dark tie. A former CIA case officer, he shared stories of spotting potential assets, recruiting, and training agents in tradecraft. Though he was a gentleman, Mr. G had the skills to break into your home, crack your safe, assess anything of value or interest, leave and walk down the street, and then visit you the next day and you would not even have a clue that he had been there. His presence and mannerisms were unremarkable and unassuming, which is what made him so good. Heck, from what I understood, his own son did not know his occupation until he was a young adult.

Our team of Greybeards, though they were difficult to work with at times, had all sacrificed a lot. Some had risked their lives to protect our country. They were totally dedicated to their craft, and I respected and admired them all. Here I was, learning from the best trained liars and spy catchers in the world.

Mr. G spent a lot of time mentoring me and helping me to navigate the world of the Greybeards. He advised me on how to deal with their hard asses when I became frustrated. I enjoyed how we worked together and appreciated everything he taught me. I learned from him how to handle people better and how to cultivate patience, even when someone was attempting to manipulate, control, or even lie to or about you. But there were times when I did get frustrated.

On one occasion, for example, one of the Greybeards with whom I was working on a project passed untruthful information about me to our principal deputy in order to cover his own mistake—directly in my presence, no less! The principal deputy became so upset he stormed off before I could even explain that it was not true. For the remainder of that day, the principal deputy avoided me, getting red in the face any time we passed one another on the floor. Up until that point, he had always been cheerful with me, without exception. I finally had the opportunity to corner him in his office the next morning to set the situation straight. He understood and eventually apologized to me, it was all worked out and we were back on good terms. Probably better terms, in fact, because I prevented him from making a potential political misstep.

But I was still livid with the greybeard who had misrepresented the truth, and I informed Mr. G. that I was totally done interacting with someone who conducted themselves in that fashion.

"I will never speak with him again," I said. "This guy could have ruined my reputation with the principal deputy."

"Why would you want to do that? Cut him off?" Mr. G. asked.

"Because I am incensed. He threw me under the bus."

"What use is that going to be? How is that going to help you?"

"I don't care. I don't need him."

"You might. What if you just kept him as your colleague? You now know who and what he is. You don't have to cut him off."

Without Mr. G's advice, I would never have spoken another word to this particular Greybeard. But I kept working with him. Now, years later, we still remain in touch and collaborate on cybersecurity-related issues.

Mr. G's advice was immensely helpful. I have always been a person of high character and integrity, and I generally find it difficult to play games, manipulate, or tell lies. But I had quickly learned that in the spy game, there is no honor among thieves. But some of the people in the game, like Mr. G., were principled. He never let on to the other Greybeards that he was advising and counseling with me. We could not have been more different, but we had a connection—though even as I write this book, I cannot be sure what the connection was. All I know is that thanks to Mr. G., I held my own, maintained my sanity, and managed to thrive, despite the inherit challenges and difficulties of our work.

Beyond the work itself, I had to navigate the office dynamics, which were competitively lethal due to the complexity of our activities and the many teams performing separate and distinct tasks. Those tasks ranged from the coordination and oversight of offensive double agent operations, to classified NSA and White House media leak investigations, to damage assessments of Edward Snowden and army specialist Chelsea Manning.

Edward Snowden was a CIA employee when he leaked highly classified information from the NSA. In June of 2013, he released thousands of classified documents to journalists. The documents revealed many global surveillance programs ran by the NSA and other intelligence agencies which had a significant impact on U.S. national security operations. The disclosures created tension between the U.S. and Brazil, France, Mexico, China, Germany, Spain, and others after they revealed that the U.S. was spying on its allies.

In July 2013, Chelsea Manning, born Bradley Manning, was convicted via court-martial of violations of the Espionage Act after disclosing nearly 750,000 classified and unclassified but sensitive documents to WikiLeaks after being turned away by the *Washington Post* and the *New York Times*.

WikiLeaks was established in 2006. It encouraged whistleblowers to submit restricted intelligence information. Manning submitted classified reports involving Iceland, Baghdad, Afghanistan, Iraq, and others. Manning was convicted on 17 of 22 charges in July

2013, including five counts of espionage and theft. She was sentenced to 35 years in prison, but her sentence was commuted in January 2017.

During my tenure at ONCIX, where personalities and individual agendas varied widely, I recall having a casual meeting with a colleague who was working on a leak investigation matter. He shared how some of those investigations were conducted, using electronic surveillance equipment and other spycraft. I left our chat thinking to myself, *I hope nothing like that ever happens to me and that I never have to be investigated.*

Working with colleagues who were or had previously been under official cover came with its own challenges. I even caught myself wondering if a blind person I noticed on the street was really blind, or if they were undercover. I could easily see how someone working in this environment long term could sink into paranoia.

Just balancing and maintaining my composure in a normal or typical work environment was hard enough, but our office dynamics raised the stakes to another level. Mental judo was the status quo. It was sometime difficult to discern a colleague's genuine intent or otherwise.

One of our first assessments involved the National Reconnaissance Office (NRO). The NRO is an agency most people have never heard of. Until 1992, even its name was classified, and the government did not officially acknowledge that it existed. Today, some activities have been declassified, but most have not. So, I have to be careful with my words.

The NRO is responsible for developing, acquiring, and operating the nation's most sensitive spy satellites. The satellites collect data, which is then analyzed and processed by the NRO. That information then gets passed along to the National Security Agency for SIGINT, as well as the National Geospatial Agency, and others. Since its inception, the NRO has specialized in using satellites to address challenging reconnaissance problems. It also delivers space-based global situational awareness for national decision makers including the president, Congress, and the director of national intelligence, and the Department of Defense.

I found myself leading many discussions and meetings with top officials on the topic of cyber threats. These meetings included rocket scientists from the Department of Defense, Department of State, and the intelligence community. We traveled to different remote locations to conduct on-site reviews and assessments, personnel interviews, and senior leadership debriefings. During one of these meetings at the State Department headquarters in downtown D.C., I recall thinking to myself how amazing it was that a kid from Cherry Street was advising some of the brightest minds in our country about cyber security threats and counterintelligence risks to NRO operations. After the successful assessment on the DEA issue mentioned at the start of the book, the greybeards and I were doing well.

Work was busy and challenging, but I decided to continue my pursuit of higher education. I registered for evening classes for graduate level courses at the George Mason School of Policy and Government. My goal was to get a second master's degree or maybe even a Ph.D. The campus was located in Arlington, Virginia, not far from where I worked and lived.

While attending an evening class, I met a very tall, smart, and supportive young lady while we were assigned to work together on a group project. Eventually, we began dating. Our relationship was a blissful whirlwind. When I was not working, we spent evenings and weekends dining out, visiting parks and landmarks, and enjoying the D.C. Metro area. I also had Washington Football Team season tickets and we would attend home games.

I lived in a quaint three-level garden-style apartment complex in my favorite D.C. suburb of Alexandria, Virginia. Yes, the same neighborhood I had lived in previously when I was stationed in D.C. in the early nineties. I love Alexandria because it is strategically located, given the challenges of commuting whether for work or leisure. I liked the neighborhood too—it was quiet, clean, well-managed, and the rent was relatively low given the location, which afforded me the opportunity to save and invest. There was just one problem.

I was beginning to have issues with noise coming from the apartment directly above me. This went on for weeks and just continued to get worse. It was so bad that I had no other alternative but to report it to the property management office on two separate occasions.

One Saturday morning, I was enjoying a late breakfast with my girlfriend as we watched the movie *Once Upon a Time in America*, a 1984 crime drama starring Robert De Niro and James Woods. The movie chronicled the lives of two best friends as they led a group of Jewish youths who eventually became prominent in New York City's world of organized crime. The film explored themes of childhood friendships, greed, betrayal, broken relationships, and the rise of mobsters in American society. It is a great movie and one of my favorite Robert De Niro films. I had originally seen it on VHS tape in Japan.

As we snuggled onto the couch and settled into the movie, all of a sudden, the loud banging and stomping sounds began. It became intolerable for at least a 30-minute stretch. The tenant rules under the lease agreement were explicit in that confronting neighbors regarding noise or other disputes was prohibited. I had abided by those rules for weeks but on this particular morning, it was really bad, and clearly the property management representatives had done nothing to address the situation. So, I asked my girlfriend to join me to speak to the neighbor with me to help reduce the potential for a confrontation.

We both threw on some sweats and went up one flight of stairs to the third floor. As we got closer, the noise grew louder and louder. It seemed my neighbor was kicking things and yelling at someone. Her voice was loud and powerful, but we could not make out what she was saying. No exaggeration, it sounded like an exorcism was taking place in the apartment. At that point, we are looking at each other thinking, *What the hell?* We began to grow concerned about my neighbor's safety.

My girlfriend was great, a ride-or-die type of person. I asked her to knock on the door and to show herself, because my neighbor was a middle-aged woman, and I thought it would reduce the possibility of a negative reaction. Heck, at this point, we were scared but she still knocked on the door. After a few minutes, there was no response. Then I knocked, this time a bit harder. One of the neighbors popped his head out of the door.

"What's going on?" he asked.

"We've been hearing some strange sounds," I said, "and we just want to make sure she's okay in there."

He nodded in understanding. "We've been hearing some crazy noises, too," he said, before closing the door.

After a few more minutes, things suddenly became quiet. I took the opportunity to knock again. We could hear someone walking toward the door. Then we heard the deadbolt unlock and the chain drag across its perch. The door swung wide open. There was my neighbor. She was a large woman, standing maybe six feet tall and weighing about 270 pounds. Her hair was in disarray and she was sweating severely. Foam leaked from the sides of her mouth. I was in shock because over the several months that she lived there, I had had a number of polite exchanges with her.

Our first instinct was to take off running—because what we were observing was not normal.

"Come on in, I never have visitors," she said in a heavy, calm voice.

The contrast threw me. It was not at all what I expected. I looked at my girlfriend, and we silently agreed to go in. We nervously stepped a couple feet into the apartment, staying close to the door. Her apartment was a red-hot mess, it looked like a tornado had blown through there. Chairs were turned over, newspapers, books, and magazines were spilled all over the floor, all the pictures on the wall were twisted around, and the apartment was dark and dreary. A total disaster zone.

She asked us what we wanted and as I began to tell her that we were trying to watch a movie and we heard loud noises, she interrupted me. "They are trying to get me, me and my son, they have satellites watching us," she said. She began pointing at various spots on the ceiling. "They're trying to get me!"

Much of what she said was incoherent, but it became clear she was talking about a spy satellite. She was convinced one was zooming in on her, watching her. We stayed and listened to her babble on for a couple minutes longer.

"Ma'am, we have to go now," I said gently.

"I'm sorry if I disturbed your movie. Thanks for visiting me." Her voice had completely changed. It switched from an incoherent babble to a kind, warm tone so fast it made the hair on the back of my neck stand up.

My girlfriend and I left the apartment in disbelief. We knew something was seriously wrong with her mentally, and we felt terrible. But we did not know what we could or should do about it.

About three weeks later, when I arrived home after work, I saw three Alexandria Police cars and an ambulance near the walkway to my building. I parked my car and began walking toward my apartment, curious about what was going on. As I reached the sidewalk, I saw emergency responders rolling my neighbor away, strapped down on a large gurney. Later, I saw a moving company loading up her furniture, clothing, and other items from her apartment.

I later discovered that she had been admitted to a psychiatric facility, which seemed to make sense given the behavior we had witnessed a few weeks before. I was never able to confirm her profession, but based on our previous interactions, she seemed to be an intelligent woman. She carried herself like many of the career government people with whom I spent my life working with. I wondered if maybe she had been part of the intelligence community. But I never knew for sure. My girlfriend and I were both saddened to hear what happened to her. We hoped she received the help she needed.

Subconsciously, I think this event made me pause and reflect. Both professionally and personally, the stress and strain of the job had begun to affect my life. Working in the human intelligence spy world was initially exciting and professionally challenging, but it was beginning to take its toll.

Life is hard enough when you are dealing with people and you know exactly who they are. You are bound to have conflicts, differences of opinion, and disagreements with your family, friends, and colleagues. That is normal. But when you work on a daily basis with people whose job it is to deflect, confuse and deceive, the stress can become intolerable.

Our organization was comprised of the top-notch personnel, the absolute best in their respective fields. Our team of greybeards was the classic example. They were superb intelligence and law enforcement officials who were all experienced spy catchers and/or security professionals.

There was one greybeard I regularly sparred with, let's just say we did not regularly intellectually agree. He was very thorough, possessed exceptional analytical and investigatory skills, and had a storied history of accomplishments throughout his counterintelligence career. His people skills on a personal level were great. He was an overall good man, a father and grandfather, and I sometimes enjoyed our conversations. But professionally, he was inflexible when it came to his opinion. He just did not budge, and that created tension between us. He believed he was always right, no matter what. We never crossed the line of unprofessionalism, but I tell you, there were times we came right up to that line.

But when I think of all our battles, most of the time I would have to give him the edge because many things did not seem to bother him like they bothered me. Stated simply, he was just head-strong, but this former master chief never backs down. Eventually I won the war.

As I recall, we were assessing an extremely sensitive and classified foreign intelligence-related cyber matter that impacted a federal department. During our work, we consistently sparred on the tone and approach of how we should document the lessons learned and recommendations for the department in our draft report.

"Stan, I think your draft analysis has too much detail and is a bit in the weeds. We should adjust this," I said.

"Well, Kenneth, I have the pen, and I think this is spot on," he responded.

"I am telling you, Stan, this is not strategic enough for the audience and more impact is needed."

Turning red-faced, he yelled, "I know what I am doing! You don't know what you're talking about, Kenneth!"

"Now I see you are making this personal, Stan. I have had enough of your antics."

After days of back and forth with Stan, I took Mr. G's advice and decided to let it all play out.

We had a meeting with the intelligence official from the department that had requested our support. The greybeards and I were assembled in the conference room, all set up for the preliminary draft review. The lights in the conference room were dim, casting a shadow on the mood before the conversation even began. The intelligence official entered the conference room eager to hear our initial findings.

She greeted us and we began with a brief overview presentation. That portion was received well, and we then had a question-and-answer session. Then she began to review the summary document we had prepared. She looked up in frustration before shouting, "You are all a bunch of Cold War warriors, this is not what I had expected, and this is not acceptable!"

As the lead of the team, I remained calm and collected, but I was ecstatic on the inside. I responded professionally.

"Ma'am, we understand your concern and will take this opportunity to reevaluate and make adjustments as appropriate, and will reschedule our preliminary debriefing," I said.

When she left the conference room, I resisted the urge to say, "I told you so." Everyone in the room understood the message. Her implication was that we were out of touch because the Cold War with Russia was clearly over, and we were now dealing with China.

That particular greybeard had needed to hear the intelligence official's assessment because he was the primary author of the draft summary report. We call this "having the pen." As a result, he was more cooperative and receptive to the changes and revisions recommended by the team because he knew we were all professionally embarrassed by the intelligence official's inflammatory comment. We then collectively revised the report to reflect the approach I had been pushing the entire time. Although I certainly derived some satisfaction from the vindication, for me, it was never entirely about winning, per se, but rather working together to produce an accurate and excellent result.

When we held the follow-up session, we passed with flying colors. Later, along with our director, principal deputy, and our team of greybeards, we debriefed eight senior officials and major stakeholders within the department on our assessment and recommendations to address the critical matter. This was well received. This was an extremely sensitive matter involving national security and remains classified until this day. I recall our director saying, "This matter is the soft underbelly that threatens our national security." His words were true then, and the issue remains a challenge for our nation today.

Our office remained busy as we focused on myriad issues involving counterintelligence, economic espionage, cybersecurity, and other emerging threats. In March 2012, we learned that instead of performing specific large-scale counterintelligence and cybersecurity risk assessments of individual federal departments and agencies, going forward, the organization would conduct strategic assessments that would provide a holistic view of the threats across the United States. These assessments would focus on key counterintelligence challenges, such as the targeting of sensitive, intellectual property, and other research information by foreign nation states, counterintelligence risks, and cybersecurity threats.

This was a budgetary decision—reduced time spent on assessments reduced the overall costs of the program. Although it made sense from a budgetary and even a technical perspective, for me and some of the greybeards, working on the individual assessments was more exciting because it meant that we had the opportunity to travel the nation, as well as to visit agencies within the local Washington D.C. Metro area conducting interviews, collecting information, preparing assessments, and debriefing senior government officials. Our tailored assessments and reports made a difference in the security postures of the respective agencies.

Migrating to the broader strategic assessments meant that now all our time was spent in the office and things just were not the same, at least for me. What used to be a dynamic and exciting environment was now almost lethargic.

Other organizational changes took place as well. Our long-time director had retired, and a new director was named. With the change in leadership, new alliances were beginning to form, and uncertainty was settling in.

Not only had these changes impacted our work culture, but I also felt it in my personal life. I had ended up pushing my girlfriend away because I had difficulty with my work-life balance. The strain of my work overwhelmed me and left little room for a personal life. Early on, she made many attempts to reconcile our relationship to no avail. I later realized how much I missed her support and care and attempted to rekindle our relationship. We finally met and had the opportunity to talk. She looked me straight in the eyes and said, "Kenneth, I love you, but you hurt me too bad."

Her look and words hit me powerfully. I felt her pain and sincerity and it changed me instantly. I made a personal commitment at that moment to never consciously hurt another human being, and I have not been the same since.

From a professional perspective, life was then somewhat easier because I focused solely on managing the office dynamics and work activities, without the added complication of a personal life. But this is not necessarily a good thing. There was just work and no life balance. This work had changed me. I had learned a lot, but wondered, was I a better person?

One morning, a few months before our organization was scheduled to move to a large highly protected and secured intelligence campus in Maryland, I arrived at the office incredibly early. There were only a few other colleagues in the entire office. When I stepped into my office, I placed my backpack on the desk like I did every morning, but something felt different. I found myself looking up at the ceiling. I then bent down on my knees and began looking under my desk. I stood up and looked around my small office and did not see anything out of place. I then sat down and had a moment of consciousness and realized that in the brief moment, I was totally paranoid.

I then began to think about my neighbor. Though clearly something was not right with her mind, she had said things that, based on my experience, were grounded in reality. What had made her lose her mind? I understood that we were capable of doing the things she had feared. I realized in that moment that something had to change. Finding myself subjected to even a brief moment of paranoia was enough to motivate me to want to change to a normal existence. I wanted to live a life outside the human intelligence spy world.

I had lost my mother and my last love. I was not going to lose my mind.

CHAPTER 15

BECOMING THE BEST VERSION OF OURSELVES

Present Day, North Bethesda, Maryland, July
2021

"What is necessary to change a person is to change his awareness of himself."
—Abraham Maslow

Illegitimate Sun chronicles my life's journey and the important lessons I have learned. Starting from a small, two-bedroom wooden house on Cherry Street, in an underprivileged neighborhood in the capital city of Columbia, South Carolina, to serving our country and working with the top counterintelligence officials in the spy world, I have defied the odds.

I have long been an admirer of Socrates, the Greek philosopher who is credited as one of the founders of Western philosophy and who expounded on the concepts of right and wrong behavior.

Socrates also believed that the *love of wisdom* was the most important pursuit for a human being, above all else. My lifelong pursuit of high character and integrity, as well as my quest for knowledge and education, can largely be attributed to having studied Socrates in junior college.

Socrates also believed that a life in which one lives under the rules of others, in a continuous routine, without examining one's own dreams and goals, is not worth living. Thus, his quote, "The unexamined life is not worth living." Those words were purportedly spoken by Socrates at his trial after he had chosen death rather than exile.

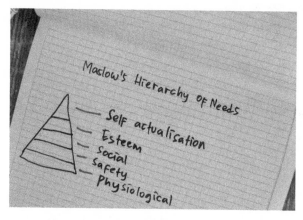

Maslow's Hierarchy of Needs.

This book, *Illegitimate Sun*, is my examined life. In examining *my* life, I discovered that life is an evolution in developing wisdom, experience, and establishing the discipline towards the fulfillment of one's greatest potential. Abraham Maslow[36] affirms that in his hierarchy of needs.

36   Abraham Maslow. https://www.simplypsychology.org/maslow.html#gsc.tab=0.

Throughout my life and career as a naval cryptologist and work with counterintelligence officials, I was inspired to write this book to give back what was given to me, the legacy of my mother's character, and to share with others the life codes I cracked during my journey. These include:

- Mistakes and failures should be options for growth
- Character and integrity are worth something
- Overcoming and defeating yourself is freedom
- Unhappiness and frustration are unproductive
- To uncover your success, you must look inside yourself and think
- Self-knowledge is personal power that leads to peace and happiness
- You cannot buy peace of mind
- Fear provides clarity and heightens our awareness
- No matter what we do in life, no one can beat you at being you
- A mother's wisdom is indisputable

Understanding who we are and developing our own self-awareness provides important insights to having a successful life.[37]

Thinking, developing my mind, managing my emotions, and practicing self-discipline were the fundamental principles that guided me. As a young boy, it was my mother's wisdom that influenced and directed my path, through the imparting of the ideas

---

37   Earl Nightingale. https://www.nightingale.com/authors/earl-nightingale.html.

of good character and integrity. Later in life, it was the mistakes, failures, education, and mentorships.

By experiencing those mistakes and failures, I learned, I grew, and I improved. I had overcome and defeated myself, and once I defeated myself, I was free to think and thrive with clarity and cultivate my own success. Through my pursuit of higher education and the support of mentors, I improved my intellectual abilities and social skills, which lay the foundation for my personal and professional achievement.

It has been nearly nine years since I left the spy world, and I have never felt more at peace. Growing up, I was determined not to conform to my circumstances. As a young African-American man being raised by a single mother who had had a limited education and had started from a working-poor environment in the segregated south, statistically the numbers suggested that I might not have made it off of Cherry Street, but here I am.

Currently, I am a member of the Senior Executive Service (SES) at a U.S. federal government agency specializing in cybersecurity risk and IT security compliance. As a cybersecurity leader and veteran naval cryptologist, I continue to build teams of cybersecurity and counterintelligence subject matter experts, thwarting hackers and uncovering vulnerabilities and risks to prevent the exposure of government computer systems and sensitive data to foreign nation state actors, criminal organizations, trusted insiders, and other adversarial cyber threats that impact our national and economic security.

Today, I consider myself a greybeard, not only because I have attained wisdom, knowledge, and experience in my professional life, but more importantly, I am now self-aware and, as a testament to my mother's memory and legacy, I have become the best version of myself and continue to strive towards my greatest potential. Something she always wanted for me and my siblings, despite our inauspicious start on Cherry Street.

DISCUSSION GUIDE

Illegitimate Sun is the true story of a naval cryptologist's journey from humble beginnings as the son of an unwed mother in the segregated south, to traveling the world and cracking the code to life's most important lessons for becoming the best version of yourself and achieving your greatest potential.

- What is the significance of the book title, Illegitimate Sun?
- What role and impact did the author's mother have on his life and career?
- What is the primary theme or themes of the book?
- What does Cherry Street signify in the story?
- What does the Greybeards represent in the story?
- How did the memoir make you reflect on your own life?
- What do you find most compelling in the author's story?
- What are your thoughts on the 10 codes the author cracked?
- Why is education important to the author and how is it being expressed?
- What are your overall thoughts on the author's journey?

CPSIA information can be obtained
at www.ICGtesting.com
Printed in the USA
LVHW091058081121
702740LV00002B/8